ABOUT THE AUTHOR

Trina Pitcher (BA, BBSc (Hons), MA (Org Psych), a seasoned psychologist, executive coach, and accomplished speaker, has dedicated over three decades to helping people and teams not only excel in the workplace but also flourish in their personal lives. With an impressive academic background – a BA, BBSc (Hons), and MA (Org Psych) – she has cultivated expertise in leadership, business, and wellbeing. Trina's impactful work has touched the lives of many hundreds of individuals, elevating their leadership skills, enhancing their business acumen, and improving their overall wellbeing. Her contributions have been pivotal in boosting their quality of life, both within and outside of the workplace. As the founder and director of Flourishing Executives, Trina offers tailored training programs and coaching services designed to empower executives, teams, and organisations to optimise their performance and wellbeing. Her extensive experience spans across a wide array of industries, where she assists leaders in cultivating cultures characterised by flourishing, resilience, and growth. Beyond her professional roles, Trina also serves as a counselling psychologist, a mentor to young women, and a valuable member of the Disaster Response Network. Her approach is firmly rooted in the latest research in positive psychology, neuroscience, and leadership, granting her a profound understanding of the challenges and opportunities that individuals, teams, and leaders confront in today's ever-evolving and demanding landscape. Trina balances her life as a mother to two teenagers, an avid runner, a self-professed chocolate enthusiast, and a dedicated practitioner of yoga. Her debut book, *7 Anchors*, is a testament to her extensive knowledge and passion for helping individuals and organisations navigate the complexities of the modern world with resilience and success.

www.flourishingexecutives.com.au

7
ANCHORS

HOW TO LEAD A GREAT LIFE, DESPITE THE SH!T THAT HAPPENS

TRINA PITCHER

FLOURISHING EXECUTIVES

Published by Flourishing Executives
Collins St, Melbourne VIC 3004
www.flourishingexecutives.com.au

Copyright © Trina Pitcher 2024

Trina Pitcher asserts their right to be known as the author of this work.

ALL RIGHTS RESERVED.

No part of this publication may be reproduced, stored in a retrieval system, or transmitted in any form by any means electronic, mechanical, photocopying, recording or otherwise without the prior consent of the publishers.

978-0-646-88286-4 (paperback)
978-0-646-88287-1 (ebook)

Book design and typesetting by Typography Studio

I acknowledge the Traditional Custodians of the lands on which I live and work. I acknowledge Traditional Custodians of Country throughout Australia and their connections to land, sea and community. I honour and respect their Elders, past, present and emerging, and extend that respect to all Aboriginal and Torres Strait Islander people.

To Penny and Archie,
who constantly inspire me to live well,
love life, and give our future hope

Contents

Foreword by Dr Arne Rubinstein — ix
Introduction — 1

PART ONE: LIFE AS WE KNOW IT

1. Change in a heartbeat — 5
2. Get ready for change — 11
3. Frame your brain — 19

PART TWO: ANCHORS IN ACTION

4. The 7 Anchor Model — 39
5. Self-Awareness — 43
6. Purpose — 83
7. Relationships — 101
8. Gratitude — 129
9. Health — 151
10. Routines — 181
11. Resilience — 209
12. Your Anchor Self — 229
    Conclusion — 235

SMART Goal Template — 237
Acknowledgements — 241
Bibliography — 243
Additional Resources — 260

Foreword

Thank you, Trina, for writing this book. It contains learnings, strategies and insights that can support anyone navigating this mysterious and complex adventure we call life.

In my work, first as a Medical Doctor and then creating transformational Rites of Passage for hundreds of thousands of people globally, I have seen one thing more than anything else. Whether it is in Australia, Sweden, America or Bhutan, whether it is with children, adults or the elderly, whether rich or poor, sick or healthy, skinny or fat, change is the common denominator. Change happens throughout our lives; it happens whether we ask for it or not. It might feel good or perhaps the worst thing in the world. Change comes with age, at work, in relationships. Change comes at the least expected times and in the most unanticipated ways.

Trina Pitcher has clearly described and given us all a path through this most basic aspect of being human. In *7 Anchors* she clearly outlines how we can create change for ourselves that is well beyond what we would naturally have imagined in our sphere of control. Some things, like how we organise our time, what we eat, whether or not we exercise and how we parent our children, come down to self-awareness, discipline and structure. This is not necessarily a new concept, but Trina gives a clear method for assessing how we are tracking in the seven fundamental areas she has identified as being critical for success. She not only gives us the tools to self-assess, but through practical tips and questions along with the use of the Learning Journal she also maps out a clear strategy for improving ourselves in each of these areas.

What particularly excites me is that Trina clearly states up-front that things won't always go well and that sh!t happens. And Trina knows this as a lived experience. She has dealt with way more than her fair share of sh!t but through walking her talk and taking all that she has learned after 25 years dealing with and observing people and organisations, she has managed to find a healthy way through.

If only this were part of the school curriculum! Imagine if all children were brought up knowing that things were not always going to be perfect, that we would all face challenges and that how we deal with challenges defines our lives more than the challenges themselves. Way, way too often I hear people making excuses about why they can't move forward in their lives, blaming other people or circumstances for their situation. People who say they will be happy when they reach a certain milestone, or they will make a change when such and such a thing happens. It is challenging and sad to see, especially when they are friends or colleagues and are stuck in a loop feeling powerless to change. In reality, there is so much they could be doing.

On the other side, I see people in incredibly challenging situations who still somehow maintain a positive outlook, take advantage of every opportunity that comes their way and smile with gratitude whenever possible. I have spent a lot of time in Sri Lanka, in a very poor area on the east coast. Never in my life have I seen people who have so little, live in such difficult circumstances, and yet smile and laugh so easily. Their attitude to life has taught me a lot about how possessions and big houses are certainly not necessary to have a happy life.

Your mindset is your fixed set of beliefs and values, that which determines the decisions that you make. With a growth mindset you can learn and improve; it is a critical 21st-century life skill. However, I have come to believe in the possibility of a Transformational Mindset. It is when we are able to open our minds in a different way to truly change.

FOREWORD

To see situations and problems that previously seemed unresolvable in a new way and find creative solutions that allow us to unlock possibilities that we may never have imagined. This book is an opportunity to create a Transformational Mindset and take ourselves to a new stage in life.

7 Anchors is not just a book to read. It is a call to action. It is an opportunity to take control of the things you can. It is also a call to action to manage in the best way possible those things that are not going to plan and are difficult to accept.

I wish that I'd had access to this book when I was a young man. It could have made a huge difference to my life.

Thank you, Trina, for writing this book.

Dr Arne Rubinstein MBBS FRACGP
CEO, The Rites of Passage Institute

Introduction

The unexamined life is not worth living.
— Socrates

Welcome to the next exciting step for living a great life. I invite you to think of this book as a guiding but slightly stern friend, part challenger, but one who is non-judgemental, and makes no assumptions. One who is curious and compassionate. This is not a book of empty promises or social media claims. Within these pages you will be given the opportunity to be honest with yourself and to receive considered guidance and advice to live and lead well, even through your challenges.

For the past 25 or so years, I have seen clients who thrive and clients who struggle. My job has been to help them all be the best humans they can be and live the best lives they can live. My job has also been to teach some of them leadership skills that benefit them personally, and their employers. It has been a privilege to witness and guide so many people to become what I would consider highly successful people – keeping in mind that my definition of success covers all aspects of life.

Over my working career, I have noticed patterns of behaviour across my clients who were thriving. Some of these people were thriving in really difficult times. The 7 Anchor Model came out of the unmistakable similarities between the behaviours and mindsets of those who thrive, regardless of whether life was great or completely sh!t.

My hope is that *7 Anchors* becomes your go-to book when times are good and bad, but mostly when you're not sure what to do next. With

INTRODUCTION

these Anchors you will start to understand that you do know your next step, you can achieve the great things you choose for yourself and you don't have to do it alone.

Read on and live life well!

Trina Pitcher

PART ONE

LIFE AS WE KNOW IT

1

Change in a heartbeat

When life hits pause

Our lives can change in a heartbeat. In 2017 I was working in Organisational Psychology and Executive Development. My kids were healthy, engaged, active and doing well at school. My ten-year-old daughter was doing ballet, swimming, triathlons and joining the rest of us for charity fun-runs. She was a sweet, compassionate, caring and talented girl with a very bright future. My nine-year-old son was sporty and thriving, with a great sense of humour and a life-loving spirit. I had wonderful relationships and loved my work. We were all in a good place.

Without warning, on Friday 10 November 2017, we suddenly found ourselves on a new trajectory. My daughter experienced her very first symptom. It was to be one of many. Before my eyes, she changed from being active and independent to a high-needs child with hindered mobility. My life hit the pause button. Doctors' appointments and regular hospital visits filled our days. I was slammed with the deep emotional turmoil of caring for my little girl who was suffering and didn't understand why. The whole family felt it. There was no time for work, cooking, cleaning or exercise. Being mum was about all I had in the tank.

About six months in it became clear that she would not recover quickly. Worse, she was continuing to deteriorate. Doctors told us it was likely she would be unwell for years. This was when I realised that we would have to find our new 'normal'. And I ambitiously wanted my new normal to include being the best mum for my kids, working at a very high standard *and* living well. It also became clear that to do this I would have to look after myself.

It was time to walk the talk. I'd been researching and working with people from all life circumstances, from high performers to people whose lives had crashed in around them. I knew the behaviours I would need to adopt, and I knew they would be effective; but *knowing* and *doing* can feel like they are on opposite sides of Sydney Harbour. So I took on the role of being my own client.

At this point, I'd love to tell you a magical cure story. Reality check: we faced setback after setback. My daughter's health became an ebb and flow of deterioration, with moments of recovery followed by further deterioration. There were days when I didn't want to face the day, and other times when I was travelling interstate for work and didn't want to come home.

Let me take you back

Let's go back a little further, so you can understand why this topic is important to me. When I was 11 years old, my mother contracted a terminal illness. I went from having a fit and active mother to one who was stopped in her tracks and caught unawares. As was the way of the time and most definitely the way of my family, no-one told me what was happening. I was a curious kid and did my best to find out. Keep in mind there was no Google back in the 1970s. I stumbled across a brochure by my mother's bedside and learned that she had a rare auto-immune condition. To my horror, it also reported that 95% of people with this condition die within the first 12 months.

Communication was so poor, I would come home from school not knowing if my mother would be home, in hospital or dead. I worried all the time. I recall one time when we weren't allowed to touch her because her bones had turned to chalk and couldn't hold her weight without risk of breaking. She had to lie still on her bed for two weeks. She was in and out of hospital, and I watched her deteriorate. She had variously been given from two weeks to three months to live on numerous occasions, but somehow she managed to get over each hurdle.

Remarkably, she beat the odds and survived long enough for the medical world to find a new medication that would help her navigate through and live a long life. A life filled with adventure and travel that lasted 89 years. She was not what you would call a loving mother, but she was, without question, the most determined person I have ever met. No hurdle was insurmountable. She proved her doctors wrong on countless occasions through her sheer grit and desire to survive.

Throughout all of this, I was lonely. There was no warmth and nurturing. My mother's energy and focus were elsewhere. She was trying to survive and if there was any energy left it was spent on my brothers or the pragmatic chores to run a household. Preparing meals for us to eat was her baseline. My father's response was to remain largely absent and to immerse himself in his work. He was a hard and very difficult man who expected us to all join him at 6 pm each night for a three-course meal. The main interaction I had with my father in my early teens was for discipline. It felt like there was no room in our house for love or peace. Happiness, joy and laughter were not on the agenda. It was a brutal time. Incredibly stressful. For my parents, with a Jewish heritage, carrying the legacy of the Holocaust and the oppression of Jews, the priorities were survivability, intelligence, and education with a portable skill.

In my family, you needed to be intelligent to be successful. Intelligence was celebrated and ever-present. I recall as a child watching one of my little cousins having to recite a long passage from Shakespeare. Poor kid. He was only about seven years old, but everyone thought he was brilliant. His parents were beaming. I came from a family of super-bright minds where intelligence was currency. My mother was a highly regarded biochemist, and my father was an anaesthetist. Full academic scholarships were plentiful. My brothers were completely on board with this – they seemed to have direction. My elder brother was clear from the age of about five that he wanted to be a doctor, just like his dad.

My other brother's purpose emerged much later, and when he found it, it gave him a lot of energy and direction for how to spend his time.

As far as I could see, though, those same super-bright adults seemed to be living miserable and socially awkward lives. As a critical teenager, this was not my idea of a great life. I loved people and had great friends. I wanted to enjoy life and have great relationships. But I was still searching for my path and my place. I spent quite a few years living recklessly (or at least my family's idea of living recklessly). What I know now, after some of my more reckless moments, is that intelligence is not enough. The ticket to a good life has many more moving parts.

Fast forward to 2020

In February 2020, Covid-19 marched around the globe. My hometown of Melbourne was no exception. We were all put into lockdown and, as it turns out, became one of the most locked-down cities in the world. I was booked to run an executive leadership transformation program over in Western Australia, and like many other people was thrown into a situation where I had to redefine how I worked. Four days before I was due to fly I was told I would have to deliver the program via Zoom – something I'd never used before.

I'd built an entire practice on being in the room with people. I like people! I ended up working in my little office in my house for all of 2020. No face-to-face client work at all. No coffees with clients, no off-sites and definitely no interstate travel. So many things I had grown to love about my job were taken away in a flash. But I had a job, and it seemed that my services were in demand. I learned that when you refuse to let go of the vision of what your life can be, it forces your focus and your timeline. My 7 Anchor Model was in its infancy and when I started building it, I had no idea I'd be testing it on myself.

Across all the people I knew, some were clearly doing better than others. I knew from the work I had been doing in the 7 Anchors Model that certain behaviours and attitudes helped and others hindered. People who were able to work on the right behaviours and mindsets kept themselves well. It became clear that those same qualities (thoughts and behaviours) I have seen in outstanding performers were the same ones helping the everyday person survive the social and economic changes of the Covid pandemic. The intensity of the situation was showing me more evidence, more quickly than I could have imagined. It was showing me that with the right mindset and behaviours, we can alleviate the challenges of working through difficulties *and* live well. It's not a binary choice.

I wrote this book to help as many people as possible to understand themselves and their choices. I want you to live a lead a great life – even through difficulty and uncertainty.

2

Get ready for change

What you will need

I'm excited that you want to live well and you are prepared to learn how to do it. We all know what it's like to start with good intentions on one day, have the enthusiasm start to wane the next day and then berate ourselves for not sticking with it. This is not one of those books! *7 Anchors* has been written for you to pick up whenever you need it, to go back and try again and again, as many times as you need to change the direction of your life.

There are a couple things you can do now to get ready for successful change:

- Make sure you've had enough to eat and drink before you start reading.
- Give yourself time and space to read.
- Read with a curious and open mind – throw your 'buts' in the bin.
- Be prepared to think about your thinking, with honesty, even if it feels confronting.
- Always treat yourself with kindness and respect.
- Trust that you can change – don't judge yourself.
- Be prepared to develop, delegate or dump the stuff that's not working.

- Oh, and pop out to the shops and buy a journal to write in – this will become your 7 Anchors Learning Journal. Choose one that is small enough for you to carry around and keep close by.

Throughout my life, my coaching conversations and my leadership programs, some themes remain constant. I share them with you in this book but change names and circumstances to protect people's privacy. Even if the names are fiction every story is real, with real people, real situations and real feelings, and the method is backed by research. I want you to have the benefit of all the things I have learned over the past 25 years so that you can choose ways to think and behave more effectively in your present situation. I want you to be bold enough to start to design the life that you want to live, what it might look like and the steps you need to get you there.

My recommendation is that you work through the book once in its entirety. If you can. If you can't, that's fine too. We all read differently. If you bought a paper copy, scribble all over it, mark those sections you know you want to come back to. Some areas you might feel that you know already. Please read them once, just to check back in with your thinking. The 7 Anchor Model is designed to enhance what you know and to remind you of what is important, to help you become more aware of what you are doing well and where you could benefit from paying attention. I want you to make choices that help you live well now and into the future.

How this book works

Make as many notes in your journal as you like. Don't wait for me to ask questions. Each chapter has exercises and questions for you to write down the answers to in your journal. You will see this little symbol ✎ frequently throughout the book, highlighting the opportunity.

As you read and work through the exercises, ask yourself:

- What is resonating for me about this?
- What is it asking me to do, think and feel differently?
- Where in my life would I like to apply this?

The 7 Anchor Model forms the backbone of this book with each Anchor connected and dependent on the others. All 7 Anchors are important; however, varying situations and circumstances will call for one Anchor more than another. Focus on what you find most useful and build outwards from there. Once you absorb the spirit of an Anchor, the specifics will sink in with practice.

Use the 7 Anchors to be your own Inner Coach. Give yourself plenty of time to let the material sink in. Find opportunities to experiment and play with it. When times are really tough, go back to basics and ask yourself: What's the one thing I can do right now to help me, or the situation I am in? The most important thing is that you take away something to make your life sustainably better. Imagine how much better off we would all be if everyone found one or two ways to live a better life!

> ### ✎ Get Ready for Change
> Thinking about your work and home life, make a list of things that:
> - could be better
> - you wish to keep
> - you wish to let go of or change.
>
> You can do this again after you have defined your seven roles in the Purpose Chapter. According to Stephen Covey, author of the best-selling book *The 7 Habits of Highly Effective People*, we have room in our lives to manage seven roles well. Each of those roles will enable you to fulfil some sort of personal purpose. Once we have identified our seven roles we are in a position to determine their needs and how we can live them fully and effectively.

How to use your Learning Journal

Make it a practice to use your Learning Journal at the end of every chapter to set yourself some new goals. It will be a place where you can jot down your notes, thoughts and ideas. It's also a place to set yourself some improvement goals.

Setting goals in your Learning Journal

When setting a goal, have a good reason behind why you want to learn and grow in the particular area. It is the rationale that will keep you going, even when you feel like you are not making any progress.

Your goals might be to:

- increase something
- make something
- improve something
- reduce something
- save something
- develop someone (yourself!).

The acronym SMART has been used to provide a guide to set goals and objectives for what you are trying to accomplish. SMART goals are used in the workplace to provide clear and mutual understanding of expected levels of performance and professional development.

Specific: What will be accomplished? What actions will you take?

Measurable: What information will measure progress and success? How much? How well?

Achievable: Is the goal doable? Do you have the necessary skills and resources?

Relevant: How does the goal align with broader goals or who you want and need to be? Why is the result important?

Time-bound: What is the time frame for accomplishing the goal?

Here's an example of a SMART goal from someone who wants to improve their performance. It also includes a milestone and a deadline, to ensure that it has measurable outcome and a time-bounded end point:

> *Description:* To grow in my career, I need to improve my PowerPoint skills. By taking online classes and reviewing tutorials, I'll improve my PowerPoint skills so that it only requires 25% of my work time.
> *Milestone*: Complete an online PowerPoint course in three months.
> *Deadline*: Next employee review in six months.

At the end of this book in the Resources section, you will find a template for writing a SMART Goal.

Success is closer than you think

When life turns to sh!t, it's hard to find the presence of mind to zoom out and look at what is happening to us. Our capacity to make good decisions seems to evaporate, and bad decisions just pile on top of each other.

We've all been there! When life can feel so hard we don't want to get out of bed, or go to work. Getting up off the couch is a major event and going for a run is what that 'other' you used to do. It feels almost impossible to make a healthy choice. You've joined the self-soothing club: food, alcohol or your 'poison' of choice. The accompanying feelings can be overwhelming: sad, sleepy, angry, disengaged, afraid, listless, unhappy, demotivated, disempowered, unsafe and even fearful. Your triggers may be many and varied. They might come from having an unwell child or perhaps difficulty with a colleague or boss. Or that feedback you received about work which was not quite up to scratch, and there were reasons that you didn't share with anyone.

Essentially, these feelings come from sh!t just happening around you. Something I like to call life! A large majority of life is outside your remit of control. What I've come to realise in my working and my personal life is that we're not taught how to cope with difficult situations and the uncomfortable feelings they bring. We are somehow expected to know what to do. Newsflash: most of us don't. So, whatever your trigger might have been and whatever your response was, it's important to know that it's okay – you weren't taught how to manage it. The good news is that you can learn to cope in these difficult situations and live well. This is where the first Anchor, Self-Awareness, becomes important. What we notice about ourselves is valuable information for how we can change our behaviour.

Yesterday was one of those days for me. Things had been very tough on the home front. I'd been terribly worried about my daughter's health. After a poor night's sleep, I woke up and felt a low-grade hum of anxiety, a slight tightness in my throat and, unsurprisingly, little energy. It was supposed to be a writing day. I had planned to spend the morning editing to get ready for a session with my writing coach in the afternoon. I sat at my desk doing absolutely nothing! I didn't even turn my computer on. But after 'wasting' some time, I started to get a read on myself. And I knew I wasn't going to get anywhere with how I was feeling unless I actively did something about it.

I could tell that the balance was tipped and my feelings were driving my behaviour. Granted, they need to be acknowledged and respected, but they don't always get to drive. Rather than beat myself up and force myself to spend time working, I knew I had to actively choose something that would give me some joy because I certainly wasn't feeling it. On the table in my office, was an unfinished jigsaw puzzle. I had grown to think of it as a distraction because I would spend my procrastination time there. To force myself to write would have been fruitless. Over time I've come to realise that sometimes you just have to recognise and accept where you are at. A far better thing to do, from a self-awareness and self-management perspective, was to choose something that made me feel better. For me, that was the jigsaw. Each time I got a piece in I genuinely felt a little bit better. The more pieces, the better I felt.

I like routine. On this day I was being hard on myself for not slipping into the routine. Every day is not the same, but each day I like to set a routine. The day before I had such a constructive day and got through everything on my calendar. This included going for a run, playing the piano, writing for about six hours, cooking dinner, feeding the kids, meditating, going to the supermarket, dropping off some jam to a neighbour, going for a walk with a girlfriend and my dog, drinking my eight cups of water and probably more. When I don't set a routine, not much happens.

When I allow myself to go with the flow it's curious to reflect on what I gravitate to. In my session with my writing coach that afternoon, he asked me a fabulous question that made me think about where my head was at that day. He asked, 'What will nourish you to maintain your creativity to continue writing this book?' I started to list them and realised that there are an awful lot. Here are some of the things on my list that I really enjoy doing:

- spending time with the kids
- writing
- working with clients
- playing the piano
- walking and playing with our dogs
- helping someone
- chatting to a neighbour
- going for a run
- walking the streets, at a park, in the forest, at the beach with a good friend
- catching up with friends (even if only by Zoom)
- spending time with my mentor
- having good enriching conversations, perhaps at my book club or in the community of Practice Sessions that I run
- reading a good book
- gardening
- making jam and giving it to my friends
- dropping a warm home-made loaf of bread to family and friends.

There is no doubt that the list is endless.

I realised that it wasn't necessarily the things on the list that were important, but that my list was so long. When I thought about it, so many things give me joy and until I reflected on this, I didn't realise that I had so many options to choose from when I'm feeling stuck. If I do just one of those activities, it's going to help me feel better. I'm not saying that it's a cure-all, but it's a start.

> ### ✎ Get Ready for Change
> In your Learning Journal, list *all* of the things you enjoy doing and the people you like to be around.
>
> Keep it close. Add to it. Refer to it when you're stuck in the sh!t.

3

Frame your brain

You've started on the path to change, so that you can live a good life when the sh!t comes your way. Your Learning Journal is fresh and ready. Now it's time to reframe some of your thinking and make sure we're on the same page when I introduce some (possibly) new concepts.

Living Well

What does living well really mean?

What your life will be like will, in part, be determined by the biological processes that are occurring in your body, most of which happen behind the scenes. In this book 'life' will mean what you are experiencing from morning to night, seven days a week for about 80 years, if you are lucky, or for even longer, if you are very fortunate. In 2017–2019, life expectancy in Australia at birth was 80.9 years for men and 85 years for women. This might seem like a narrow perspective when compared to the much more exalted views of life that myths and religions tell us, including promises of the afterlife and so forth. However, to me it seems that the best strategy is to assume that the 80 or so years is our only chance to experience our world, and we should make the fullest use of it.

The quality of life – what you do and how you feel about it – will determine whether it is a great life. And that will be directly determined by your thoughts and emotions and how you interpret them. Take some time to consider what living well looks like. We need to reflect on some parts of life that are so firmly embedded in our minds and habits and shift how we think about them. Living well is about sustaining what is good and eliminating the not so good. It's about taking the external pressures – political, economic, social, technological, legal and environmental – and managing our responses to them.

Our lives *will* be controlled externally – people will take advantage of us and take as much of our energy as possible for their own agenda (which is why it is so vital to learn to say 'No'). This happens time and again in the workplace, where people are often pushed to their absolute maximum. And, in some regards, rightly so – that's how a good business needs to operate. It makes no business sense to utilise an employee at half capacity. Living well demands that we participate in life with clarity of purpose, capability and communication.

I have now devoted over 20 years of my career searching for patterns of behaviours that lead people to live well. Having worked across all sectors of the workforce (corporate, federal, state and local government, not-for-profit, health, education), I've come to the view that my clients see success as gaining and maintaining balance in their lives. Balance between challenge and easefulness. They also talk about great relationships and living with purpose and authenticity. In listening to these people, I have been trying to determine what differentiates really successful people from the rest.

Living well needs a belief and a reason to do it. It needs to be sustainable because we want it to last for as long as possible! It needs a very good reason sitting behind it. I believe it is everyone's birthright to live a great life. I want it for me and for my family. I value it. I am willing to fight to live well, even though life for our family has been frickin' hard. I am fortunate to have two beautiful kids. I want them to have a great life. So, as their mum, I need to lead by example. I am motivated by my clear reason for wanting to live well.

One of the keys to success is that I'm not waiting to be motivated. No-one will knock on my front door to remind me to live well. In line with the thinking of Simon Sinek, our 'Why' becomes crucial because it drives us. We fall back on our 'Why' when things become difficult.

There is no end to what you can accomplish with a clear 'Why'. Here are a few of my personal 'Whys':

1. So that I can be a present engaged, happy, healthy mum to my kids, to give them every chance to grow up as vital, independent, engaged, connected, happy and healthy humans
2. So that I feel nourished, challenged and happy, and enjoy life
3. So that I contribute and make a difference to others in a positive way
4. So that I can be a positive role model to others, showing that it is possible to live well, even though life can be very hard at times
5. So that I have a reason to get out of bed in the morning
6. So that I can fulfil my purpose for being on this planet – to help others to live and lead well in work and in life – to flourish
7. Because the alternative fills me with dread.

While we reframe our brains to think about living well, it's also important to think about success. The definition of success has been different for each and every one of my clients. The media bombards us with different ideas of success. Friends and family play their role in shaping our ideas too. We might think that success is extrinsically measured: promotion, recognition, status, financial stability, wealth. But when we scratch little deeper, other intrinsic things seem to bubble up.

The work perspective gets merged with the life outside of work. Success starts to include getting home at night to spend quality time with family – husband/wife/partner, the kids, grandchildren – and girlfriends/mates. Going on a holiday. Getting that game of golf. Finding the time to read a book! You could do a vox pop and get a hundred different descriptions of success. You might also receive different answers from the same people on different days.

In my estimation we are truly successful, when we:

- feel in control
- make living a great life our priority
- live in line with our values
- feel as if we are the manager of our own destiny
- feel in balance, and importantly,
- know how to navigate through difficulties.

I have learned to live each day as it presents itself and to adjust my sails accordingly. I still have a True North. I know where I am going, but I am also willing to do side trips and go off course, if that is what is required of me. I know what success looks like for me. As I write this I find myself a little off to the side, waiting for things to settle. My beautiful daughter's illness is ever present and at times overwhelming. It is extremely taxing and she needs constant monitoring. But she is well looked after and will be okay with the right management strategy. Even though life can be so hard, I have seen that there is a way to navigate through the bad and to live well.

> ✎ **Frame your Brain**
> Take some time out to answer these in your journal:
> - What does your great life look like?
> - What do you hope to get out of this book?
> - What specific areas do you need to focus on?
> - What do you have the energy to start with first?

Difficulty

Difficulty is a part of our lives.

And it's more important than you think. It gives us perspective. It builds our resilience. It's a normal part of growing up. Knowing that we can overcome obstacles and learn from our struggles lays a solid foundation for success in life. Facing challenges forces us, in a helpful way, to work with others. When difficulties are faced or conquered, we feel a wonderful sense of accomplishment. When the next hard time hits, we draw upon the previous to get us through. It tests us. It can make us question our reason for being or provide a reason for being. When we face extreme challenges and find ourselves 'living' in survival mode, our goals and values feel irrelevant. But they are not. To hold on to hopes and dreams with a realistic blend of hope and optimism gives us a reason to fight. To be hopeless is to lose those dreams and wishes.

When difficulty strikes, it's easier to shut down communications. None of us has been taught how to talk about the hard stuff. I had a client – let's call her Jane. I had been working with Jane as both a coach and a consultant for her organisation for some years and I knew her very well. Her husband of close to 20 years became extremely unwell and was hospitalised for what seemed to be unusual symptoms. They were very much in love and Jane, understandably, was very worried about him. Throughout this time, I kept in close contact with her. After he had been hospitalised for a number of weeks it seemed as though things were looking up. There was even discussion of him being discharged the following week.

To my utter surprise, the very next week I received a message from Jane that her beloved husband had passed away. It was a total shock. For everybody. We talked about the importance of Jane looking after herself, to which she replied: I just don't know how to do that! And I know she meant it. She didn't know the basic steps to care for herself in a time of crisis and mourning. Moreover, she hadn't discussed the difficulties she was facing with anyone other than me. In hard times, we often lose that clarity and the wherewithal to maintain ourselves functionally. We neglect our sleep. We often feel less hungry, or for some, food is comfort, so we eat more and make poor food choices. This might feel and even be okay in the short term, but as a long-term strategy it doesn't hold.

Jane and I had talked about the importance of when and how to communicate with her organisation, so they could support her. This was important for both parties so that she could be where she needed to be without feeling guilty. Sometimes that meant being at work, rather than the presumption that she should be beside her husband all the time. She needed a guilt-free break from her husband's reality too! I noticed that Jane was struggling to manage herself and her workload. This was quite understandable. She loved her job and didn't want to leave it but as time went on, being physically and mentally available at work became progressively more challenging. Jane's friends, family and work colleagues also didn't know what to say or do around her.

In Western society we don't openly face conversations around difficulty, death or dying. Our culture keeps adversity at a nice, safe distance. Death is a process left to hospitals and funeral parlours. At work, we defer to HR staff for the challenging conversations. These positions have their role, but as humans we have a responsibility to look out for and care for others, and sometimes that includes difficult conversations.

The surgeon and writer Atul Gawande has said that our reluctance to honestly examine the experience of ageing and dying has increased the harm we inflict on people and denied them the basic comforts they most need. From what I have seen, this holds true in everyday life. It has led to a vacuum of the skills that are needed to navigate the tricky situations. The impact of not having conversations about difficulties denies people the opportunity to get access to the resources and support they most need. If we notice someone isn't doing so well, or we know that they are having a hard time at home, surely we can and should ask: 'Are you okay? Do you need anything?'

The conversations about 'difficult' don't really happen. And when they do, we don't do them terribly well. People are far more at ease talking about their successes and wins. After all, we reward the wins, right? Plus, most of us want to give the impression that we are doing okay. Difficult is uncomfortable and the dialogue seems to shut down. Most of the time when you ask someone how they are, they will tell you they are good, even if they are not. We all know that difficulty is part of people's lives. It seems crazy to me that we don't talk about it. Even crazier is the idea that we will just know what to do and say, even though it's not taught in school or at work. We are not on this planet alone, so why try to navigate through as if we are?!

Feeling Stuck

Who is in control of you? If not you then who?
—Dr Seuss

The language we use to describe ourselves can either liberate us or limit our capabilities. It can move us forward or keep us still. I saw my mother fight tooth and nail against the limits she was expected to accept by her disease and the doctors. She had a steely determination to push her own boundaries. Her mindset was incredible. She refused point blank to be stuck.

I recall a client coming in to see me, and when I asked her how she was, she looked at me in all seriousness and told me that she was paralysed – even though moments earlier I had seen her walk in the room, pull out a chair and sit down. In her mind, she felt paralysed. It was restricting what she felt she was able to do and yet it was only a belief. It was not a truth.

There's an old allegory about a baby elephant that was tied to a fence post. The baby elephant learns that even after trying, it can't move beyond a certain distance from the post because of the rope. When the baby elephant grows into a big strong elephant and is easily able to walk away from the tether, it doesn't. It has grown up believing that the rope is unbreakable. In psychology we call this learned helplessness. It is strongly linked to self-efficacy: our belief in our innate ability to achieve goals. How we view ourselves either allows us to utilise our capabilities or not.

If you think you are paralysed, whether it's true or not, it is going to impact significantly on what you allow yourself to do. Another way of looking at this is as our limiting beliefs, where our belief system, regardless of the truth, hampers our behaviours. They are thoughts and opinions that we believe to be true. They can impact us negatively as they stop us from moving forward and growing. Essentially, they prevent us from pursuing our goals and desires. It can be helpful to tap into liberating beliefs. We do this by challenging all those limiting beliefs and asking ourselves what we would do if none of them were true.

When we allow our beliefs to grow, we open up room in our lives for ambition. I had a friend when I was growing up called Pluto. He was a funny, uncomplicated guy. He loved performing in front of people and making them laugh. He made a living as a clown. Nothing wrong with that. He was clear on what he wanted to do with his life. Brilliant! On the outside, it looked like he'd set himself up for success. He gathered substantial crowds for his street performances. He also gained the occasional paid job. That was all fine in our late teens and early 20s. As the years rolled by, it became clear that Pluto was not ambitious.

I'd occasionally bumped into him at a children's party, wedding or bar mitzvah. For me, seeing him was like stepping back in time. It was as if a line had been drawn in the sand and the distance between us drew farther and farther apart as time progressed. As time went on it became more evident that he had not changed, developed or grown. I'm not exactly sure why that was. His work as a clown remained simple and uncomplicated. He remained living in the same dingy warehouse that he shared with various other people who came and went. He never settled into any sort of relationship. Back in the early years, his future seemed pretty bright. But over time, it dimmed. I'm not exactly sure why, but it was as if he never launched.

In stark contrast to Pluto are the many hundreds of clients I have worked with who have ambition. They wanted to grow and change. They have had the motivation and determination to strive for their goals even in the face of failure and adversity. It is both constructive and life-affirming. They have chosen to improve, overcome and face up to their challenges. Each and every one of them has wanted to be, in some shape or form, better.

The best way to tap into what you need to do when you are feeling stuck is to think about your Best Self: when you are being your best, what are you doing; what would others see you do? Then it's about taking one of those behaviours and putting them into action now – so you can get there – to your best self. I have a friend who wanted (and did) win gold three times at the Olympics. To help him get there every little thing he did, right down to brushing his teeth with a gold toothbrush, was in line with a way of thinking and behaving to get him there – to his goal, to his Best Self.

> ### ✎ Frame your Brain
> Take some time out to answer these in your Learning Journal:
> - What are some of the dreams you had that you may now have let go of?
> - What assumptions are you making that may be limiting you today to reach your dreams?
> - How would you describe your Best Self?
> - What are you willing to do to be more like your Best Self?
> - Take action and start today to put as many of those Best Self behaviours in action!

Everyday Grind

Life can get in the way of having a great life.

We have both external and internal interruptions vying for our attention. Some we can control, others we can't (or perhaps not fully). External interruptions are those that you have no control over, such as the weather, a grumpy boss or Covid-19. Others may include:

- unwell parents or children
- your car breaking down
- somebody needing to do the dishes before you can serve dinner
- somebody having to submit a report so you can get an approval to go ahead on a project
- the traffic
- the kids needing you to go to after-school sport
- an urgent meeting being called, which you have to attend
- your phone ringing
- a toothache, which is distracting and requires a visit to the dentist
- your boss walking in and asking if you've 'got a minute?'

You get the idea.

Internal interruptions are the things we do have control over. Like how we choose to spend our time and who we choose to spend it with. They include:

- having an 'always-on' behaviour, particularly around our devices
- poor decisions, such as saying 'yes' when we should say 'no', or saying 'no' when we should say 'yes'
- feeling out of control and feeling stressed
- doing too much or not doing enough
- feeling negative and pessimistic
- not having a goal or drive and feeling stuck
- letting ourselves get too tired, hungry, thirsty.

Together, these interruptions form the push and pull of the everyday grind.

When you know who you are, you can understand your skills and capabilities and use them to sustainably manage what the everyday grind throws at you. Using careful discipline you can keep the promises you make to yourself. You need to consciously determine how you act toward yourself. We all need to treat ourselves like someone we are responsible for helping. The 7 Anchor Model helps you get in touch with the things you have control over: your understanding of your strengths and weaknesses, your health, your relationships, your routines.

🔖 Frame your Brain

Change starts with a quick audit. Setting a clear understanding of where you are at now. Take some time out to check in with yourself and answer the following questions in your Learning Journal:

What is the current state of my:
- Relationships
- Health
- Sleep quality
- Diet quality?

What is the current state of my work:
- Am I using my skills and abilities?
- Am I challenged enough?
- What are my gaps?

Now, think about the possibilities of life:
- What might my life look like if I cared for myself properly?
- What career would challenge me, allow me to be productive and help me contribute to a positive future?
  If I could do anything for a living, what would that be?
- What would I be doing if my body was healthy and strong?
- How would I expand my knowledge?

Choice

*The sooner you make a choice,
the sooner you can make a commitment.*

—James Clear

The very first step in leading a great life is choosing to do so. It's not just going to happen. It needs to be in the diary! The choice to live a great life, though, must also be driven by your 'Why' – your rationale for wanting to live a great life. I have had several pivot points in my life where I realised a choice needed to be made. A more recent point for me was after my marriage ended. I realised that I was miserable and quite lonely. Again, it was not where imagined I would be at that point in my life. I still wanted to have a great life and I needed to live well for my kids. I also realised that I had no time to waste. The time to start working on it was right then. I had to work out what a great life would look like for me.

For reasons that will be made clear later in this book, our brains are wired to make us look for the negatives. I was feeling pretty sorry for myself. As a very comfortable 49-year-old mother of two young children, I had to pick up and 'start again'. My first instinct was to be bitter and angry about my life. I didn't like the sound of that, so I had to find a replacement behaviour. The replacement and opposite of bitter/angry/crappy for me is to live and lead a great life, being happy and grateful. It is impossible to live a great life if you feel bitter and angry! So, as far as I could see my only option was to live a great life.

We all need to make choices around our routines, our habits, how we look after our health and our minds. Quite possibly, the most valuable thing to learn is that even when it feels as if you don't have a choice, you *do* have a choice. Be aware of your mindset and ask yourself if you want to choose to live a great life. Once you become aware of the reality and abundance of choice, you will realise that you have more power in any situation than you thought you had.

> ✎ **Frame your Brain**
> Listen to the language you choose to describe yourself. Take some time out to answer the following questions in your Learning Journal:
> - How are you seeing yourself right now? Choose a few words. How would you describe you to you?
> - How would somebody sitting next to you describe now? Do you like what they are seeing?
> - If you could change one or two things so they see you more positively, what would they be?
> - Could you start to adopt those changes now?
> - Choose a word or two to get a glimpse of how you're seeing yourself.
> - Is it positive, is it enabling? Is it going to move you forward or hold you back?
> - Choose another word or two to capture how you would like to see yourself.
> - Think about some small things that you could do today to help you get closer to how you would like to see yourself.

Capture the sorts of things you would like to incorporate in your great life, and what that looks like for you and what it would feel like.

Change

> *The world as we have created it is a process of our thinking.*
> *It cannot be changed without changing our thinking.*
> —Albert Einstein

At the risk of being infuriating – to change something, you need to change. You can't keep doing things the same way and expect change. To shift an old behaviour and integrate a new one can be difficult. But hey, we've talked about difficult, right? Difficult is something you can manage – you're probably already doing it. So, let's just change the type of difficult. Most important is your reason to change. It needs to be a good one. No good reason, no good change. If we have a good reason for change, our reason pushes us through the emotional and routine resistance. It gives us the resolve to keep pushing and changing. We are, after all, creatures of habit and emotional beings.

Remember, there is always a cost for inaction. It helps to be aware of the advantages that change can bring you. They need to far outweigh the disadvantages of continuing with the way things are currently. Think deeply about the pros and cons of a potential change, so that it resonates deep down in your bones. It will help you remember when the going gets tough.

Think about timing but don't use it as an excuse. I've had many conversations with clients who tell me that they want to make changes but the timing doesn't work. I've heard things like, 'I can't have that difficult conversation with them at the moment, they've got so much going on!' Or, from the person who is doing the work of their team, 'I can't delegate to my staff at the moment, they have too much to do.' The first question I would encourage you to ask yourself is this: if not now, when? And the second question is: how bad does it have to get?

Across all stages of change we move through an emotional response. It can feel similar to the stages of grief.* Here is a simple three-stage change model:

Step 1: Awareness Becoming aware that some sort of change needs to occur. This could be internally or externally driven. It might be a change to do with you – about your thinking or your behaviour. Or a change that is happening around you or to you. If we stay in this stage for too long, we tend to go into 'pause' mode. The new information does not feel real and we become paralysed by the uncertainty.

Step 2: Acceptance Accepting that the change is going to happen whether we like it or not. This is the moment we realise that some sort of (personal) cost is involved, and we will need to do and be something different. This is the stage where the magic happens. As we come to terms with the reality of the change, we start to put ideas together of 'what, when and how' we could 'think, do and say' differently to align ourselves with the change. We are able to explore options and consider putting new plans in place. This is where the change begins. Grief expert David Kessler explains that when we accept our situation, we find our power and regain control, because we are no longer fighting the truth (Kübler-Ross, E., & Kessler, D., 2005). Part of this may involve planning. The when, what and how, and the think, do and say, need to be done differently. This is where innovation occurs. We can find new ways of being and doing and (re)align our choices with our values and purpose. At this point, anything is possible. From here we move into meaningful action.

Step 3: Action Where the rubber hits the road and we move from thoughts to doing and commitment. We have the opportunity to create a positive outcome by putting into action the 'what, when and how' you could 'think, do and say' from Step 2. Momentum begins to take hold and we regain our confidence. We make fewer assumptions, we begin achieving again, and personal and/or professional growth happens. We become filled with hope, even though life is still challenging and uncertain.

You will have heard people say, 'Just get over it!' The social timer goes off and someone decides that you just need to jump the puddle and move on. It doesn't recognise the pain and challenge of a situation. If we just jump over that bit, we miss the opportunity for learning and adapting. Perhaps this is why we're not very good at grieving for the loss of others in Western culture. Accepting that a change has occurred acknowledges the difficulty of the loss while we move forward with our lives. When we authentically accept what's happening around us or to us, it makes room for our brains to open up and seek new possibilities.

Explainer
* Back in 1969, Elisabeth Kübler-Ross coined the five Stages of Grief:

> **Stage 1:** Shock and denial – a state of disbelief and numbed feelings. Often feelings of isolation, avoidance, confusion, elation, alarm and fear.
>
> **Stage 2:** Anger – as the reality sets in, there may be frustration, irritation and anxiety. The anger may be directed to individuals. For example, politicians are to blame for not handling the spread of Covid properly or cruise liners are dangerous Covid cesspits.
>
> **Stage 3:** Bargaining – struggling to find meaning, reaching out to others, and finding comfort in telling our story. A Covid example would be: 'If only we hadn't used that security firm to manage our hotel quarantine.'
>
> **Stage 4:** Depression – feeling overwhelmed, helpless, hostile and seeking flight. Worrying about the costs, material and immaterial, or both.
>
> **Stage 5:** Acceptance and hope – this phase is marked by withdrawal and calm.

Micromoves

It's easy to think that big change needs big moves. If, for example, we want to lose weight our goal could be to drop 10 kg, which is a fairly ambitious goal. But when we break it down and consider a more realistic weight loss of, say, 250 g a week, we can see that we are on the path to losing 1 kg a month. Rather than sign up to a reality TV weight-loss show, we might just need to cut out one unhealthy component in our diet. That seems more achievable. I had one client who substituted his regular can of Coke with water. He would drink a can every lunch and dinner, sometimes even two. When we did the maths, it turned out he was consuming 2250 calories per week on Coke. When he decided to replace the Coke his total sugar intake for the week reduced significantly, adding up to a 117,000-calorie reduction in one year.

When I sat down to write this book, the idea of it felt very overwhelming. Again, using micromoves, I broke down the writing into a number of words that I felt I could achieve each week. That weekly word target became my focus for a solid six months, resulting in many thousands of words written. What starts as a small win or a minor setback accumulates over time into something much more. This can be applied in all areas of life.

I had another client who received feedback that he was both unapproachable and unfriendly. It turned out that he was painfully shy. He knew he needed to build more connections with the people he worked with but didn't know how to go about it. The whole thing caused him a lot of anxiety. So, we applied the micromove approach. He started by looking for opportunities to be more helpful. He did things such as hold open the door when someone was coming through. If he was going out for a coffee, he'd see if anyone else wanted one in the office. He gave eye contact and said hello when someone walked past. Over time people started noticing and were kinder and warmer towards him. He, in turn, gained more confidence and began to open up.

Micromoves are smaller tweaks and gestures that we can feasibly incorporate into our daily practice so that over time they add up to significant change. According to Steve Jordon, an *Omaha World-Herald* staff writer, when Warren Buffett was asked by a student at a Columbia University investing class what he could do now to prepare for an investing career, Buffett reached for a stack of trade publications and papers and said, 'Read 500 pages like this every day… That's how knowledge works. It builds up, like compound interest.' With compound interest, your investment over time (in this case, behaviour) increases exponentially.

From a relationships perspective, when you invest positively in relationships, people are willing to invest positively in you. Being a little more considerate each and every time you're with someone can build loads of positive relationships all at the same time. The same goes with learning a new skill – think about adding just a little every day. This year I took up the piano again, after not playing since I was 14 years old.

Over the year I have practised almost daily, and my piano playing has increased well beyond my expectations.

Once you feel you have incorporated a particular micromove into your daily practice, you can add another one. Build it up!

> ✎ **Frame your Brain**
> What are your change goals?
> - Take some time out in your Learning Journal to make a list of things that you want to improve.
> - What would you like to do more of?
> - What would you like to do less of?

PART TWO

ANCHORS IN ACTION

4

The 7 Anchor Model

One of the most exciting things I discovered as I was developing the 7 Anchor Model was that the behaviours, thoughts and skills you learn while using it are valuable for all of life's challenges. This means that no matter what type of difficulty life throws your way, you will have a toolkit that helps – every time. This is powerful.

The beauty of the 7 Anchor Model is that it is immediately recognisable and usable. Each of the Anchors may be taken and worked on individually, but they come together as an algorithm to form an Anchor-Self Profile. The 7 Anchors have emerged from my own lived experience, from research and client experiences. The more experienced you become with them, the more valuable they become. Each Anchor acts as a reminder to keep us in check. And each of us will find that we are more experienced and comfortable with some Anchors and less comfortable with others. Some people will have brilliant Relationships, but when it comes to Routines they spin in circles. That's fine: we are all different.

Find your balance with the 7 Anchor Model. You'll no doubt be doing quite well in some areas; these will likely be strengths of yours. In other areas, you might need to pay more attention; these are your development opportunities. The reason the 7 Anchor Model works in all situations is because the importance weighting of each Anchor changes along with the circumstances. Some situations might require considerable focus on the Relationships Anchor, while another situation would require attention to the Purpose Anchor.

We all need all 7 Anchors. Strengthening your weaker Anchors, to bring about balance, will help you live and lead a sustainably better life. As you make your way through each Anchor, you will start to understand that some feel naturally easy, and others more confronting. Don't be afraid of the confronting Anchors. This is where the gold can be mined – the very start of your positive change.

7 ANCHORS

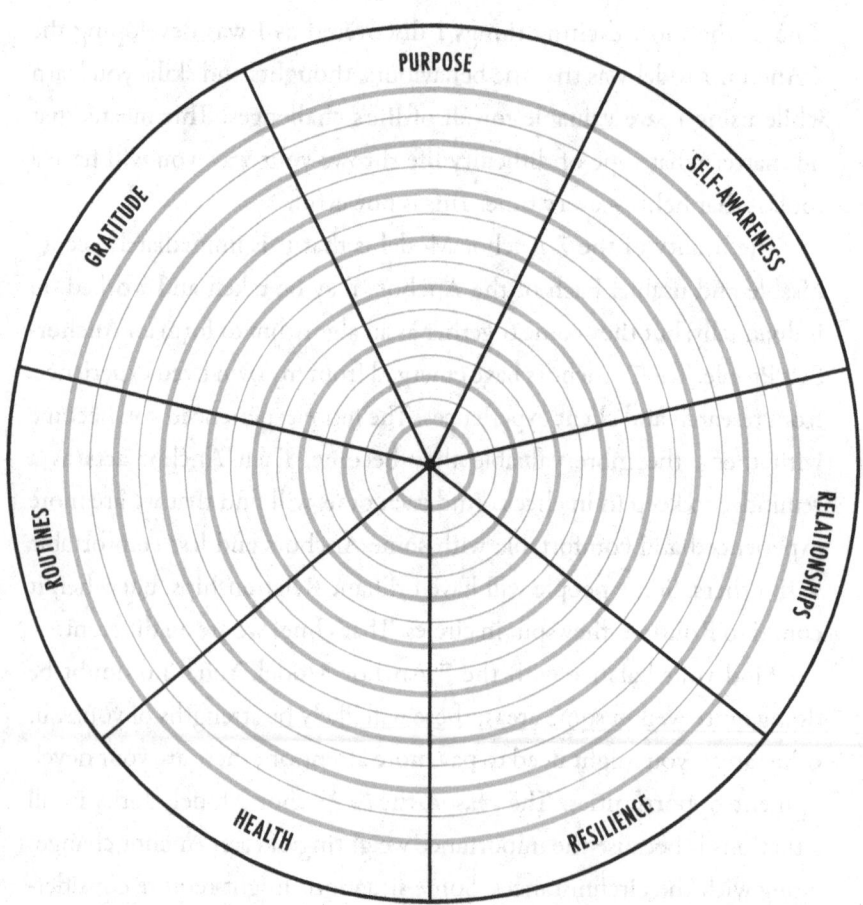

Self-awareness: an accurate and clear understanding of yourself, including your values, attitudes, thoughts and behaviours, and how you manage yourself in line with your needs.

Purpose: a clearly articulated purpose where you seek to contribute to and improve situations for yourself and others.

Relationships: maintaining strong positive relationships with yourself and others, both at work and in your personal life.

Gratitude: a feeling of thankfulness towards the world, or towards specific individuals for what they have, without constantly seeking more.

Health: a state of complete and balanced emotional and physical well-being.

Routines: an organised routine that eliminates unnecessary decision-making, bad habits, actions and tasks, and makes room for bigger, more critical thinking in line with who you want to be.

Resilience: responding well to the pressures and demands of daily life.

At the end of each Anchor you will find an Anchor Self-assessment. Spend some time completing this for a clear idea on how well-developed each Anchor is in your life. At the end of the book, these individual Anchor scores can be translated across to form your Anchor Self-profile.

5

Self-Awareness

One can have no smaller or greater mastery than mastery of oneself.
—Leonardo da Vinci

Self-Awareness is a vital anchor to help you navigate well through life, especially in difficult times. In this chapter I explore why it is so important and yet not that easy to build. It's one thing to know that you're feeling angry and why, completely another to know what to do next. I'll also give you some strategies for managing what you do discover once you become self-aware. You will learn about emotions, feelings, values, and the many internal and external things that affect your behaviour. But most importantly, you will learn how to build and develop self-awareness.

Why is Self-Awareness important?

Torn between two places
Let me take you back to a Monday evening when I was in Sydney for the start of a three-day work trip. The kids, nine and ten years old, were being looked after by their dad back in Melbourne. At this point, my daughter had been very unwell for a couple of months and we were still trying to work out what was wrong. On this day he took our daughter to see a rheumatologist, well regarded for her expertise in diagnosing and treating musculoskeletal conditions and autoimmune diseases. It was

5.30 pm when my phone rang. I was just about to go out on an evening run with a girlfriend. I almost let it go to voicemail but saw that it was from home and wanted to know how the appointment went. The doctor had assessed our daughter and recommended, without giving us a diagnosis, that for the best chance of recovery, we should put her to bed, keep her still and limit her movement for at least several weeks. While I was trying to register what I was hearing, I felt a flush of emotion. Thoughts started rushing through me: how could we even do that; how could she manage being perfectly still for several weeks?! My heart was breaking. It became hard to think. Here I was, a thousand kilometres from home, about to run a three-day leadership program, knowing my daughter had just been told that news. She's unwell and afraid and her mother was not there. The guilt I felt was excruciating.

I had so much to consider and resolve. I knew I was not up for making any decisions. In the flood of my mind, I needed time to think. My reality looked like this:

1. My friend had been waiting in the hotel foyer for me for some time now
2. I was, up until 15 minutes ago, about to go on a run around Sydney Harbour
3. I had 24 participants relying on me to run a three-day program starting tomorrow, some of whom had been waiting months to get on it
4. I had a daughter back home who wanted her mum
5. She was safe and well, being looked after by her dad
6. I had a raft of really uncomfortable feelings and emotions to deal with
7. I needed courage but I felt dreadful.

When my head cleared enough I had to tap into my self-awareness. I reminded myself of a rule of thumb that I have relied on time and time again: to not make major decisions when I feel overwhelmed. Knowing that running makes me feel better and often helps me to process my thoughts, I went for that run. I'd been looking forward to the joy of running around Sydney (okay, I accept that one person's joy is another person's torture, but this was definitely joy for me). The run would buy me some thinking time, help me put things into perspective and burn off some adrenaline. I also had the support of my friend to talk through my options. I had a commitment to 24 people who had no idea about my change in circumstance. I reminded myself of who I want to be as a person (see Purpose Anchor). My work is vital to me. It enables me to help other people be better. It also recharges me, so that I can go home and be the fully present mum I need to be. Nothing was going to change in the next few days so, with the blessing of everyone back home, I decided to stay on and run the program. I'd be home in a few days.

To get myself into work-mode the morning of Day 1, I had to compartmentalise 'Trina at work' from 'mum-mode'. I told the person I was running the program with what was going on at home and of my decision to stay. His response of compassion and support was amazing. I had an ally to let me know if I was at all off my game. Without sharing, I would have missed out on vital support. This is something I have learned over and again. My relationships are crucial to me. I let the participants know (very briefly) what was happening so they could see that, despite everything, my choice was to be there with them. I wanted them to see the value of the program as an opportunity to grow their leadership capability, to learn and be better. From my perspective, these 24 people were our future leaders, and my role was, in some small way, to help them get there.

Managing through this situation involved no less than four of the 7 Anchors:

- Self-Awareness – I needed to read and understand how I was feeling and have some confidence that I would find a way to be true to my values and manage my way through (even though it may be scary and hugely challenging).

- Relationships – I needed the support of my family, friends and colleagues. I would have really struggled going through this on my own.
- Purpose – I had to keep in check who I am as a person and keep that in mind to help with my decisions.
- Health – I was not going to be okay if I didn't look after myself.

How Self-Awareness helps

Self-Awareness is about knowing who you are. It helps you choose what you are meant to be doing in that very moment. It's about finding ways to manage yourself to be at your best in a situation. Managing these moments, in the moment, so that you can make a difference to your future self. All we can control is who we are and how we (choose to) act in this very moment, with the guidance of our values (what's important). Our Self-Awareness Anchor helps us do this.

Self-Awareness is present when you understand your own emotions and their impact on your performance. You know what you're feeling and where those feelings come from, and whether those feelings help or hinder what you're trying to accomplish. You have a deep understanding of your strengths and limitations, as well as an accurate understanding of how others see you. Self-Awareness gives you clarity about who you are, your values and your sense of purpose. And with all of this on board, you are equipped for better decision-making on what you ought to be doing in your life and what you need to be doing right now. The great news is that you will also be better at knowing when an opportunity is a good fit and how to make the best of it.

We have both internal and external self-awareness (Eurich, T., 2018). The internal includes how accurately we know ourselves, and being aware of our patterns. External self-awareness is about understanding how others view us. This is the consistent behaviour that makes up your personality. It aids the rationale and builds the confidence to say 'No', enabling you to stay focused on what you are meant to be doing. It allows you to keep your boundaries in check and to maintain your personal integrity. It removes the things that are distracting you from your goals and helps you live in line with your values.

Self-Awareness at work

The Self-Awareness Anchor plays a crucial role in my leadership development programs. Self-aware leaders know when their (negative) emotions are impacting on their work, or on the people around them. They also have the capacity to deal with the challenges of their emotions effectively, by being open to feedback and willing to try alternative approaches to find better solutions.

All of us – leaders, colleagues, peers, direct reports, stakeholders and customers – need to know more about our own personalities, preferences and styles in order to better understand why we behave in certain ways. But it goes beyond just understanding ourselves. If we look at how we interact with people who have different preferences, beliefs, values and styles, it's not surprising to discover how easily these differences can spark conflict. When a leader or a colleague loses control, the consequences for the organisation, in terms of productivity, morale and engagement, can be disastrous. Self-awareness at work gives us the opportunity to learn how to respond in ways that will enhance productivity and relationships, and reduce the destructive impact of conflict.

A lack of self-awareness at work may see a person labelled as arrogant, mean or inaccessible. They might appear difficult to engage with or 'cross the line' without even realising. We all have a different set of behavioural and thinking preferences that inform how we do what we do. And they're unique to us, like our fingerprints. Naturally, we prefer some and avoid others – think conflict avoidance, for example. Adapting to the differing styles that are available to us, rather than just choosing our favoured set of behaviours will help us to be more effective across the range of situations that we encounter.

Learning to adapt requires two things: awareness of ourselves, and the ability to accurately read the people we are with and the situation we are in. People who wish to get the best outcome put personal preferences aside, modify their choices and behaviours to suit the situation. They know how they are likely to react to others and find ways and methods to manage themselves well. It's not about suppression of emotions, it's about recognising them and reading the signs, allowing you to bend, flex and process before impacting negatively on others. It also includes being mindful of how to handle yourself with others – in meetings or when receiving tricky feedback, for example.

Having self-awareness at work relies on being confident in what you can and can't do, and gives you a more accurate sense of when to reach out for help. Knowing when you need to take time out before you behave in a way that is not appropriate. When you are open to your flaws and to receiving feedback you put yourself in a position to improve. You can work from that place, leveraging your strengths, and developing or delegating weaknesses.

Mr I-Don't-Know-Myself

Or Mr IDKM, for short. A client from several years ago, who worked in a large multinational firm. He was in a high-pressured sales role, dealing in six-figure contract negotiations with major supply chains across the country. His role was moderately high-profile, but he was far from the top of his tree and he knew it. He had been in his current role for a few years but was restless and looking for a promotion, internally or elsewhere. The company, however, wasn't quite ready to promote him. When they told me of their concerns I learned, on the one hand, that they valued him because he was a high performer, winning excellent work and creating a tidy profit for the business. On the other, they were concerned that he regularly demonstrated some pretty poor behaviours, particularly in and around the office. He was often rude and abrasive, intolerant and irritable. He would lose his temper and had a reputation for leaving behind a trail of bruised people. As far as they were concerned a promotion would appear as if they were condoning his poor interactions with others. For that reason alone, they were not willing to promote him. They'd fire him

SELF-AWARENESS

if his behaviour didn't improve. And that's where I came in. If I could help him change his behaviour, they were willing to reconsider.

The first time we met we had a long debrief/coaching session. I had a lot of data from the raft of assessments he'd completed and the story was sending me mixed messages. I went into the session with an open mind. Long sessions gave us the luxury of exploring some of the 'out-of-work story' to get a sense of what was important and what might be hindering success at work. I learned about Mr IDKM's family and, more particularly, his son who was developmentally delayed and had behavioural issues. I learned how much time he needed to (willingly) spend with his son. He described the boating, fishing, four-wheel driving, camping they did together. He sounded like a highly involved dad – loving, patient and supportive. I also found him to be a genuinely nice guy, even though his workplace assessments told a *very* different story.

His data indicated that he was very hard-working and delivered excellent results. On the other side, comments from his colleagues, peers and direct reports were scathing, describing him as rude, curt and abrupt. As the session went on, it became quickly apparent that he had no idea how negatively he had been impacting those around him. What struck me though, was his response. He wasn't arrogant. He wasn't even dismissive. He was genuinely shocked and upset. He demonstrated a high level of authentic discomfort when he learned about how others experienced him.

He is not alone. Many of my clients do not stop to consider the impact they are having on those around them, and it is not entirely their fault. Organisations use reward metrics such as productivity, dollars in and dollars out. Self-awareness and impact are not used as metrics of success in a business. He had no idea of his impact because he'd never stopped to find out and no-one had ever given him that feedback … until now. The session ended well, with one of his goals to engage me as his coach to help him with his unpleasant and destructive behaviour. My objective was to build his self-awareness and his ability to self-manage.

Where to start? Just how much did he know about himself? I began with asking him about what his hot buttons were. It turned out, he had absolutely no idea. Then I asked him what his values and strengths were. Again, he had no idea. He could recite the company values, but he said they were just words to him and had no further meaning or impact on his thoughts or behaviour. In his eyes, he was just a hard-working Aussie bloke who did a good job. And let's be clear, he had been handsomely rewarded for it up to this point. He knew he lost his temper at times, but said he just got frustrated when people didn't do what he'd asked of them. Only two things in life were important to him: his family and doing well at work.

Our work together helped uncover his values and strengths and mapped out some goals. We also identified his hot buttons (more on them later) and explored what he was like when he was triggered by them at work. He was horrified that people were scared of him. He came to see that he behaved differently at work to home – a handy clue that this wasn't about capability, it was about choice and permission.

Once he started to know himself better, he learned that he could manage himself better at work too. He saw value in being curious about who he was. He began to think before he acted. He learned about the value of workplace relationships and that it's not all about the numbers or the task. He also realised that he was not working in a command-and-control business. As his relationships improved, so did his results, because he was bringing people along and getting their discretionary effort. People were far less scared of him.

After a lot of work and consistency, his reputation was completely renewed and he became a mentor to other high-potential staff within the business. He gained several internal promotions, eventually reporting directly to the CEO. Remember, this was the guy who was on the cusp of losing his job when we first met. These days I can happily say that he has become a successful C-suite executive. He faced up to who he was and did all that he could to be better.

What the research says
Self-awareness is a solid predictor of success in life. Boom! There you have it.

SELF-AWARENESS

It is the most necessary building block of emotional intelligence. We can't self-regulate without it, nor can we build strong social skills. It is a vital factor for strong and healthy relationships in all parts of life because it improves our ability to communicate (see Relationships Anchor). When we see ourselves clearly it increases our confidence and job performance, we get better work and more promotions. We are seen as better leaders; people like to work for us and with us.

Interesting fact: introverts have been found to be more likely than extroverts to use self-awareness to avoid unpleasant situations. And people with higher self-awareness have also been found to be more creative.

Tasha Eurich's research on self-awareness found that it is associated with higher job and relationship satisfaction, personal and social control and happiness; it is negatively related to anxiety, stress and depression. She also found that people who know how others see them are more skilled at empathy and taking the perspective of others. Leaders who had an accurate assessment of how others saw them (i.e. with their employees) tended to have better relationships with them, felt more satisfied with them, and also saw them as generally more effective.

Earlier on I talked about traditional intelligence and how (in my family anyway) it didn't appear to equate with a great life. People around me were bright, but they didn't always appear to be successful. Some didn't seem to 'fit in' socially and I wouldn't have necessarily called them happy. Howard Gardner in 1983 introduced the concept of multiple intelligences which included both interpersonal intelligence (the capacity to understand the intentions, motivations and desires of other people) and intrapersonal intelligence (the capacity to understand oneself, to appreciate one's feelings, fears and motivations).

At university I learned about emotional intelligence (EI) and decided to dedicate my Master's to determining the link between EI and job performance. In 1998, the *Harvard Business Review* published an article called 'What Makes a Leader?' It described the importance of EI in leadership success and cited several studies demonstrating EI as the distinguishing factor between great leaders and mediocre ones. There has been plenty of other research since that supports this.

Many organisations have realised that both academic and EI skills are needed to stand out in today's competitive business world (O'Boyle et al., 2011). Recent literature places emotions at the centre of leadership. It's now some 25 years since Emotional Intelligence came to the fore, and it is firmly accepted as a key contributor to workplace success, reduction in burnout and positive life outcomes (Miao, Humphrey and Qian, 2018; Law et al., 2008; Gong, Chen and Wang, 2019). It makes sense that those who have a greater EI navigate better through life and its difficulties by the simple fact that they are able to recognise the emotions at play and have the wherewithal to lead themselves, and potentially others, through. So, why am I talking about EI here? Because at the core of EI is the Self-Awareness Anchor.

On my leadership development programs, when I ask people what they think emotional intelligence is, they tell me it's about having intelligence about our emotions and other people's. Popular definitions refer to things such as motivation, empathy, sociability, warmth and optimism (Mayer et al., 2001). Since its inception, many models of emotional intelligence have been developed. What they all have in common is that emotional intelligence development requires a lot of engagement with your own emotions and the emotions of others.

Self-Awareness Toolkit

Topics covered:
- paying attention
- negativity bias
- emotions aren't feelings
- holding thoughts and feelings lightly
- emotional hot buttons
- managing anxiety
- values and character strengths
- scripts and self-efficacy.

Paying attention

Paying attention to your Self-Awareness Anchor gives you the opportunity to look at yourself objectively and avoid getting into situations that don't match the life you want. In practical terms, self-awareness is about monitoring the stresses, thoughts, emotions and beliefs that impact your choice of behaviour. Because ultimately, we all choose our own behaviour. It's about switching off auto-pilot mode to check in on why you are doing what you're doing and feeling the way you are feeling.

Life tests us constantly. What allows us to live and lead a great life is determined by how we navigate through those challenges, what we learn from them, and what we know about ourselves. The Self-Awareness Anchor is about having a clear understanding and recognition of who you are: your character, values, passions, emotions and feelings, your likes, dislikes, hot buttons and aspirations, and how your environment and other people impact you. When you are self-aware you know how you impact on others.

I regularly have my clients ask themselves two questions:

1. I'm doing this right now – should I be?
2. Am I where I'm needed right now, and if not, why not?

To develop self-awareness there is an inherent assumption that you are willing to ask questions of yourself and be open to the answers.

> ### Self-Awareness in Action
> Take a few minutes now to see if you can answer the following questions in your Learning Journal:
> - Are you aware of your strengths and weaknesses?
> - Can you name your top operating strengths or competencies?

We are the sum of our decisions, which are informed by our thoughts and beliefs. These come from our experiences (both positive and negative); the people we meet (our parents, teachers, friends etc.); social media; our personality; and our various intelligences, values, motives and passions. Sitting in this space are the stories we tell ourselves and what we believe about ourselves. These stories and experiences impact on our current thoughts and beliefs, and the choices we make in this moment.

Think about it: why are you doing what you're doing right now? What are the values, if any, that sit behind you reading this right now?

Most of our stories sit within our non-conscious minds (our internal dialogue). By understanding them (and their power) we become aware of why we make the choices we do. If we look back we can resurface them and bring them into the conscious part of our minds. And this is when we can question where those thoughts, beliefs, scripts and patterns of behaviour come from. And decide if they still apply today. Perhaps the most important question is: do these stories and the choices they offer lead me to the future I desire, or do they get in the way? Oftentimes, they come from a place to either keep us safe or rewarded.

Negativity bias

'The bad stuff is easier to believe. You ever notice that?' says Julia Roberts' character, Vivian, in *Pretty Woman* (1990).

We are all wired to search for the negative at a ratio of five to one. When I think about my childhood, I find it difficult to recall any positive events, yet I have no trouble remembering the negative experiences. I know for a fact that this memory belies the truth, because there were many positive experiences. Unfortunately, the negative memories tend to take up most of our thinking time. Even when we do think of joys, they are fleeting. When we get a pay rise, research tells us that the feeling of joy abates within a few months and we are then on the search for the next pay rise.

Why is it that a good day has no lasting affect? What is it about a bad day that carries over? It is what psychologists call a 'negativity bias'.

We process negative information faster and more thoroughly than positive information. Plus, it affects us longer. Of all our cognitive biases, the negative bias might have the greatest influence on whether or not we get to live a great life, but we can turn the ratio towards a more positive mindset. And you guessed it, we can do it through building self-awareness.

Listening more consciously to how we talk to ourselves (that voice in our head) and not allowing the negative self-talk to dominate is a good first step. Hire your inner coach. Give them a more distinct voice. Your inner coach can thank your inner critic for their opinion, and help you find ways to be kind and compassionate to yourself.

Around the 16-kilometre mark of a half-marathon there's a well-known hard patch. With about five kilometres to go your mind starts to play tricks on you. The negativity bias is loud and clear. Despite all of my training leading up to the event, I hear, 'You should stop. You're tired. Who do you think you are, running such distances! You're not going to make it.' However, as soon as I notice this dialogue, I can bring in my inner coach who will say, 'Wow, not even a Parkrun to go! Amazing. Enjoy this. You're fit and strong and I know you can do this. C'mon. Push.'

When we consider the facts over the fears, we can conquer the negativity bias.

Another strategy to help neutralise the negativity bias is to practise savouring the positives and the good in life (more on that in the Gratitude Anchor). Fred Bryant and Joseph Veroff (2007) define savouring as, "… noticing and appreciating the positive aspects of life … (by) paying conscious attention to the experience of pleasure.' Savouring is an important mechanism through which we derive happiness from positive events (Paul, E., et al., 2012). When we savour, we attempt to fully feel, enjoy and extend our positive experiences from the past, present or future. It turns our attention from external experience to an internal one. When we savour, we either maintain or enhance our mood just by noticing and thinking about the positive experience. Negativity bias is neutralised. Plus, we get a little burst of dopamine as we relive the positive event in our brains.

> ### ✎ Self-Awareness in Action
> Take some time out in your Learning Journal and do the following:
> 1. Think back and name five positive experiences from your own childhood.
> 2. Name three positive events that happened for you in the past week.
> 3. Think about the best day of your life: where were you, how did you feel?

Emotions aren't feelings

There is a difference between emotions and feelings. Yes, they're related, but they are quite different to each other. Emotions are associated with bodily reactions that are activated through neurotransmitters and hormones released by the brain. They are physical and instinctive, instantly prompting reactions to threat, reward, and everything in between. These reactions can be measured objectively by pupil dilation, skin conductance, brain activity, heart rate and facial expressions. The six primary emotions are happiness, surprise, fear, sadness, disgust and anger. As we mature, we acquire social emotions such as embarrassment, jealousy, guilt, shame and pride.

Feelings, on the other hand, are the conscious experience of emotional reactions. In other words, we are aware of them. When we stop and pay attention to them, we understand how we feel. Feelings are sparked by emotions and shaped by personal experiences, beliefs, memories, and thoughts linked to that particular emotion. A key differentiator between feelings and emotions is that feelings are experienced consciously, while emotions manifest either consciously or subconsciously.

Humans need emotions. They are involved in every aspect of our lives, or at least they ought to be. They help us make complex decisions and inform our judgements, whether we realise it or not. They focus our attention, make things easier to remember, and even play a big role in our social and moral development. They are a window into our values and reflect back to us what's important. They significantly impact our self-concept. Most people will have experienced the six primary emotions before they learn to talk. According to Paul Ekman (1992), the six basic emotions are Happiness, Sadness, Fear, Disgust, Anger and Surprise.

Happiness, the only positive emotion of the six primary emotions, is painted to be the golden advantage. This is driven largely by the tendency to think that we've got 'good' emotions (the ones we want) and 'bad' emotions (the ones we don't want). Both positive and negative emotions are a fundamental part of who we are; they express our basic intelligence and energy. They offer us crucial information to manage ourselves; if we ignore or suppress how we feel we turn off the information tap.

Understanding the emotions of others enables us to truly know where someone is at. When I run leadership programs I ask participants to tell me how they're feeling. The majority of us are notoriously reluctant to say and share how we feel, and when we try to, we don't seem to have the vocabulary. It's important to increase our emotional language. It is intriguing to discover the range of emotions that others are feeling. When we honestly let someone know how we feel, we are allowing them to do the same to us. According to Daniel Goleman, in dialogue with the Dalai Lama, there are 34,000 distinguishable feelings (Goleman, 2014).

Emotions are not directives

Anger does not give us permission to run around yelling. We can think about what our emotions are telling us, but they don't have to drive our behaviour. We own our emotions; they don't own us. Emotions are also quick. They don't always give us a chance to consider the best options available to us. Victor Frankl describes the idea that between stimulus and response there is a space. And in that space is our power to choose. In that choice lies our growth and freedom. In a moment I will talk about later on, when my daughter was distressed and wanted me to take her home (the stimulus), the space in between gave me the choice to assess my options and review what was important. Ultimately, I chose a response in line with who I thought she needed to be and could be. Being self-aware enabled us both to create the pause that allowed us to think about who we wanted to be in that situation.

Holding thoughts and feelings lightly

It's very easy to get 'hooked' by our negative thoughts and feelings and for them to then drive our behaviour. For example, if you're feeling angry at what someone said to you at work, you may find yourself lashing out either physically, verbally, or both! Similarly, you may be waiting to be motivated to go out for that run. So, until that happens, you don't go. Or you may tell yourself that you're not good enough or don't belong, so you find yourself behaving as if you are not good enough and don't put yourself up for a promotion or a piece of work. This way of being won't get you the results you're looking for, in terms of being your best self or allowing yourself to grow as a person. What we need to do instead is to be mindful of our thoughts and feelings, invite them along, and then act in line with our values.

When we are clear on who we want to be (our best self) then we have guidelines for what we need to do in that moment. But this will only happen if you question what you need to do in that moment! So, to be the person you want to be, to get you to your best self, you will need to let your values be your guide. Moreover, invite the feelings and negative thoughts to come along, to sit on your shoulder, but do not let them take over. You can even say, 'Hey, I am noticing that I am having the thought that I am angry, but I am going to be kind and compassionate in my response.' The idea is to hold your negative thoughts and feelings lightly and to not let them drive your behaviour.

SELF-AWARENESS

> ### ✎ Self-Awareness in Action
>
> It's time to tap into your feelings and emotions. A great place to learn is by building your feeling-words vocabulary.
>
> Overleaf there are a few to get you started from Tom Drummond's *Vocabulary of Emotions* (2021).
>
> Can you find and name how you feel?
>
> In your Learning Journal, write down some words to describe how you feel.
>
> Name some values and behaviours that will allow you to hold one of your negative feelings lightly and still behave in line with your best self
>
> TIP: You can't use 'good' or facts. The words have to be feeling words.

Showing the right kind of emotion at the right time is a powerful means of communication anywhere and it requires the emotional intelligence I talked about back in the *What the research says section*. The skill is in being able to modulate your emotions and express them appropriately. Daniel Goleman's (2007) definition of EI is helpful here: 'The capacity for recognising our own feelings and those of others, for motivating ourselves, for managing emotions well in ourselves and in our relationships.' To become confident in sharing your emotions, you first need to do a personal check-in with how you are feeling and which emotions are at play. Labelling your emotions helps identify their source and cause, which in turn helps us understand them and speed up our capacity to manage them. We can also identify the value that the emotion is pointing to and identify what it is telling us.

VOCABULARY OF EMOTIONS/FEELINGS

	HAPPINESS	CARING	DEPRESSION	INADEQUATE	FEAR
STRONG	Delighted	Adoring	Alienated	Blemished	Appalled
	Ebullient	Ardent	Barren	Broken	Desperate
	Ecstatic	Cherishing	Beaten	Crippled	Distressed
	Elated	Compassionate	Bleak	Damaged	Frightened
	Energetic	Crazy about	Dejected	Feeble	Horrified
	Enthusiastic	Devoted	Oppressed	Finished	Intimidated
	Euphoric	Doting	Desolate	Flawed	Panicky
	Excited	Fervent	Despondent	Helpless	Paralysed
	Exhilarated	Idolising	Dismal	Impotent	Petrified
	Overjoyed	Infatuated	Empty	Inferior	Shocked
	Thrilled	Passionate	Gloomy	Invalid	Terrified
	Tickled pink	Wild about	Grieved	Powerless	Terror-stricken
	Turned on	Worshipful	Grim	Useless	Wrecked
	Vibrant	Zealous	Hopeless	Washed up	
	Zippy		In despair	Whipped	
			Woeful	Worthless	
			Worried	Zero	
MEDIUM	Aglow	Admiring	Awful	Ailing	Afraid
	Buoyant	Affectionate	Blue	Defeated	Alarmed
	Cheerful	Attached	Crestfallen	Deficient	Apprehensive
	Elevated	Fond	Demoralised	Dopey	Awkward
	Gleeful	Fond of	Devalued	Feeble	Defensive
	Happy	Huggy	Discouraged	Helpless	Fearful
	In high spirits	Kind	Spirited	Impaired	Fidgety
	Jovial	Kind-hearted	Distressed	Imperfect	Fretful
	Light-hearted	Loving	Downcast	Incapable	Jumpy
	Lively	Partial	Downhearted	Incompetent	Nervous
	Merry	Soft on	Fed up	Incomplete	Scared
	Riding high	Sympathetic	Lost	Ineffective	Shaky
	Sparkling Up	Tender	Melancholy	Inept	Skittish
		Trusting	Miserable	Insignificant	Spineless
		Warm-hearted	Regretful	Lacking	Taut
			Rotten	Lame	Threatened
			Sorrow	Overwhelmed	Troubled
			Tearful	Small	Wired
			Upset	Substandard	
			Weepy	Unimportant	
LIGHT	Contented	Appreciative	Blah	Dry	Anxious
	Cool	Attentive	Disappointed	Incomplete	Careful
	Fine	Considerate	Down	Meagre	Cautious
	Genial	Friendly	Funk	Puny	Disquieted
	Glad	Interested in	Glum	Tenuous	Goose-bumpy
	Gratified	Kind	Low	Tiny	Shy
	Keen	Like	Moody	Uncertain	Tense
	Pleasant	Respecting	Morose	Unconvincing	Timid
	Pleased	Thoughtful	Sombre	Unsure	Uneasy
	Satisfied	Tolerant	Subdued	Weak	Unsure
	Serene	Warm toward	Uncomfortable	Wishful	Watchful
	Sunny	Yielding	Unhappy		Worried

CONFUSION	HURT	ANGER	LONELINESS	REMORSE
Baffled	Abused	Affronted	Abandoned	Abashed
Befuddled	Aching	Belligerent	Black	Debased
Chaotic	Anguished	Bitter	Cut off	Degraded
Confounded	Crushed	Burned up	Deserted	Delinquent
Confused	Degraded	Enraged	Destroyed	Depraved
Flustered	Destroyed	Fuming	Empty	Disgraced
Rattled	Devastated	Furious	Forsaken	Evil
Reeling	Discarded	Heated	Isolated	Exposed
Shocked	Disgraced	Incensed	Marooned	Humiliated
Shook up	Forsaken	Infuriated	Neglected	Judged
Speechless	Humiliated	Outraged	Ostracised	Mortified
Startled	Mocked	Provoked	Outcast	Shamed
Stumped	Punished	Seething	Rejected	Sinful
Stunned	Rejected	Storming	Shunned	Wicked
Taken aback	Ridiculed	Truculent		Wrong
Thrown	Ruined	Vengeful		
Trapped	Scorned	Vindictive		
Ambivalent	Belittled	Aggravated	Alienated	Apologetic
Bewildered	Cheapened	Annoyed	Alone	Ashamed
Blurred	Criticised	Antagonistic	Apart	Contrite
Disconcerted	Damaged	Crabby	Cheerless	Crestfallen
Disordered	Depreciated	Cranky	Companionless	Culpable
Disorganised	Devalued	Exasperated	Dejected	Demeaned
Disquieted	Discredited	Fuming	Despondent	Downhearted
Disturbed	Distressed	Grouchy	Estranged	Flustered
Dizzy	Impaired	Hostile	Excluded	Guilty
Foggy	Injured	Ill-tempered	Left out	Penitent
Frozen	Maligned	Indignant	Leftover	Regretful
Frustrated	Marred	Irate	Lonely	Remorseful
Misled	Miffed	Irritated	Oppressed	Repentant
Mistaken	Mistreated	Offended	Uncherished	Shamefaced
Misunderstood	Resentful	Ratty		Sorrowful
Mixed up	Tortured	Resentful		Sorry
Perplexed	Troubled	Sore		
Puzzled	Wounded	Spiteful		
Troubled		Testy		
		Ticked off		
Distracted	Annoyed	Bugged	Blue	Bashful
Uncertain	Let down	Chagrined	Detached	Blushing
Uncomfortable	Minimised	Dismayed	Discouraged	Chagrined
Undecided	Neglected	Galled	Distant	Chastened
Unsettled	Put away	Grim	Insulated	Embarrassed
Unsure	Put down	Impatient	Melancholy	Hesitant
	Rueful	Irked	Remote	Humble
	Tender	Petulant	Separate	Meek
	Touched	Resentful	Withdrawn	Sheepish
	Unhappy	Sullen		
	Used	Uptight		

Source: tomdrummond.com

> ### ✎ Self-Awareness in Action
> This exercise is designed to help you find out about the feelings and emotions of various people in your life, at work or at home.
>
> 1. Ask a few people a day how they're feeling. Take a mental note of what they say and see what you can do to modify your behaviour given how they are feeling.
> 2. If they respond with 'good', perhaps you could try again by saying, 'No, really, how are you feeling?'
>
> TIPS: Be sure to hang around so they can answer you honestly. Be authentic. Make sure you are really listening and have a reasonable and empathetic response when they do tell you how they feel. If they don't have the feeling vocabulary in their personal toolkit, then you may like to reflect back your observation of how you think they may be feeling: for example, 'Oh, I see. It's just that you seem ... today. Is that right?' You'll know if you're on the money or not. They'll either agree with you or modify your suggestion.

According to Harvard Medical School psychologist Susan David, our emotions are signposts to things we care most about. In the workplace this might be growth, recognition or a value such as trust or integrity. If your needs are not being met, negative feelings may emerge because you are not 'feeling enough of something that is important to you'. David recommends that we ask ourselves questions such as:

- What values are these emotions pointing to?
- What is this emotion telling me?
- What is it that I am experiencing here?

Doing so, enables us to start to take steps towards those values.

Emotional hot buttons

Everyone has 'hot buttons'. They're our tender spots. When we are so irritated, hurt, or angry, we feel we have to respond. And typically we don't respond very well. We might ruminate, become bitterly disappointed, bite back, retreat, or even get aggressive. A key to preventing hot buttons from messing up your day is your Self-Awareness Anchor. It helps you identify what your triggers are and what makes you feel stressed, angry or defensive.

There's nothing rational or considered about a response that comes from a hot button. It's pure emotion linked to strong values that can be triggered by specific events or circumstances. Most of the time values are quiet and unobtrusive, but when triggered they can take over and direct your behaviour. You can see hot buttons in action whenever people start to talk about 'matters of principle' or become angry over something that seems unimportant. You'll know you were acting under the influence of a hot button when you regret what you did or said the moment you cool off. The words just popped out, you turned away and slammed the door behind you. You didn't think about it until afterwards. Press someone's hot button and something will happen.

At work, according to Capobianco et al. (1999), there are nine prevalent upsetting behaviours that occur when people are:

1. Unreliable: miss deadlines or can't be counted on.
2. Overly analytical: focus too much on minor issues or are perfectionists.
3. Unappreciative: fail to give credit to others or seldom praise good performance.
4. Aloof: isolate themselves, do not seek input or are hard to approach.
5. Micro-managing: constantly monitor and check up on the work of others.
6. Self-centred: believe they are always correct or care only about themselves.

7. Abrasive: are arrogant, sarcastic and demanding.
8. Untrustworthy: exploit others, take undeserved credit or cannot be trusted.
9. Hostile: lose their temper, become angry, or yell at others.

Understanding our own hot buttons can help us avoid being thrown off balance. It gives us a self-aware moment to pause and assess our actions.

> ### ✎ Self-Awareness in Action
> Do the following hot button exercise in your Learning Journal:
>
> 1. List the nine hot-buttons out and rate which ones are a trigger for you.
> 2. Think carefully about times you can recall where you acted or spoke in haste and regretted it afterwards. Write down what triggered the response. Was it something someone said? Or something they did? Be as specific as you can.
> 3. Look for patterns. Does the same trigger come up several times?
> 4. Try replaying one or two especially volatile occasions in your head. Check your emotions as you go along. When did you start to get irritated? Or upset?
> 5. Ask close friends, partners or colleagues about what they know makes you instantly grumpy or difficult. What have they learned to avoid so they don't 'set you off'?

Hot buttons are closely linked to our fight-or-flight response, designed to keep us out of physical danger. Fast-forward to today, when the nature of threats has changed but the response is still the same. When we are triggered by emotions like fear, anxiety, aggression and anger, the amygdala* in our brain activates and sends out signals to release stress hormones that prepare our body to fight or run away. Daniel Goleman calls this an amygdala hijack. This may result in a sudden, at times illogical or irrational, over-reaction to the situation. The amygdala also disables the frontal lobes, the rational-thinking part of our brain, preparing us for fight-or-flight. Without your frontal lobes functioning adequately, rational decisions disappear.

For this reason, it's important to know how much stress we can handle before we get to our tipping point of the amygdala taking over. The good news is that through increasing our self-awareness we can get in early and avoid this response. In Malcolm Gladwell's book *Outliers*, he talks about the idea that it takes seven consecutive errors (possibly minor, human errors) for a major event to occur, such as a plane to crash. This got me thinking about human behaviour and how many minor errors are needed to reach our tipping point and experience amygdala hijack. We've been conditioned to look out for those big red flags but, from my observations, what undoes us is the accumulation of a number of small events. The obvious things are being too tired, hungry or thirsty. But there are many other potential stress factors in life: poor relationships (long- or short-term), lack of exercise, poor diet, too much alcohol and so on. It's not difficult to find seven small things to push us over the edge. Many of us are teetering on the edge of having an amygdala hijack without even knowing it.

It's good to know that when a threat is moderate, the frontal lobes have the ability to override the amygdala, leaving you to respond in the most rational, appropriate way. You can stop the hijack by using self-awareness to consciously activate your prefrontal cortex (PFC)**, but it does take some practice. Below is a three-step process to help build self-awareness in stressful situations:

Step 1: acknowledge that you feel threatened or stressed and that your fight-or-flight response has been activated.

Step 2: become aware of how you are feeling.

Step 3: ask yourself what emotions and physical responses occurred leading up to this moment.

It's okay to be emotional: it's what makes us human. Only when we acknowledge our full range of emotions and our hot buttons can we manage them. Here are some tips for doing this.

Managing emotions

Notice and name is a process of noticing the emotion and consciously giving it a name. FMRI studies show that the cognitive brain is engaged when a person makes the effort to notice the emotion and fish around in their head for a name, description or metaphor. The naming process deactivates the amygdala and reactivates the prefrontal cortex. Your reactivity is calmed and conscious processing returns.

Reappraisal. This is another conscious process that may be useful after you notice and name the emotion. Once you calm down, ask yourself if there is another way of viewing the situation. If you're struggling to find a different perspective, you're not looking hard enough. This also engages your prefrontal cortex so that the amygdala begins to quiet. Describe the situation as if you were on the outside: it helps you to be more objective and rational.

Be mindful of the emotions in your body. When we allow ourselves to notice the physical reactions (tight, shaky, rushing, raised heartbeat, sweaty hands, shaky knees, increased breathing) we can choose ways to create a safer place for ourselves. Paying attention to your body re-establishes equilibrium faster.

Remove yourself from the situation to buy some more time. If you can, stand up and walk away. Make an excuse or just say you need more time before you can continue the conversation. You're not as stuck as you think you are.

Breathe.

Explainer

* The **amygdala** is a collection of cells near the base of your brain and is part of the brain's limbic system. It's key to how you process strong emotions like fear and pleasure. It's where our emotions are given meaning and our emotional memories are formed.

** The frontal lobes are the two large areas at the front of your brain. They're part of the **prefrontal cortex**, which is a newer, rational and more advanced brain system. This is where thinking, reasoning, decision-making and planning happen. The frontal lobes allow you to process and think about your emotions. You can then manage these emotions and determine a logical response. Unlike the automatic response of the amygdala the response to fear from your frontal lobes is consciously controlled by you.

✎ Self-Awareness in Action

Learn more about your reactions to stress. Take some time to write your answers in your Learning Journal.

1. How do I react to stress in my life?
   a. How does it impact on my ability to cope?
   b. What happens to my concentration?
   c. How am I with others around me when I am stressed? How do I feel?
   d. What are my levels of energy and motivation?
   e. When do I react emotionally?
   f. When do I have a cognitive reaction?
   g. When do I react with a problem-solving mindset?
   h. Of the above three, when am I the most effective?

2. What sorts of situations events and triggers create stress for me?
   a. Is it work-based? Workload? Relationships with colleagues? Work-life balance?
   b. Is it financial?
   c. Is it time pressure?
   d. Is it physical? Lack of sleep? Lack of exercise?
   e. Is it relationships? Personal? Family? Self-expectations and personal pressures?
   f. It could be all of the above, or something different.
3. When I am stressed, be it through work or life pressures, how well do I use my social network to support me?
4. How do I react to conflict and pressure around me? Am I able to express my thoughts and feelings with others?
5. What strengths and skills do I have to cope effectively with stress pressure and life's challenges?
6. What are some examples where I have successfully coped with work/life challenges? What other experiences have I witnessed that I have learned from to cope with stress?
7. After looking at my responses to the above questions, how confident do I feel about my own ability to handle future challenges? Do they help me feel more hopeful about the future and my ability to cope well?

Managing anxiety

Unless you have reached Zen-level mastery of body and mind, life's challenges will trigger anxiety at some point. A dear friend describes anxiety as the difference between what you think you can do and what's expected of you. The bigger the gap, the greater the anxiety. And it is our body's natural response to stress. How well we deal with it will largely be determined by our level of self-awareness. Ordinary anxiety is a normal part of life; it comes and goes and doesn't interfere significantly with everyday life. The underlying concern is that we won't cope (well) with what's ahead. For some, this can be debilitating. When we are self-aware, we can read our emotions accurately and understand what they are telling us. They are providing us with the information we need to manage ourselves effectively in any given moment.

My daughter was supposed to be returning to school after having been away for three months due to ill health. The plan was for her to go for a short time in the afternoon. At 1.30 pm, I was to drop her off in reception, where she would be accompanied by the Learning Support Officer for the afternoon. When we got there, it became very clear that she didn't want to be there. She wouldn't get out of the car. It was heartbreaking seeing her in such distress and concern. She wanted me to take her home.

In that moment, I ran through our options in my head. The way I saw it was that we could go home and be dictated to by my daughter's emotions, *or* we could find a way to get her to class, in line with the value of getting an education. I knew that she would eventually feel better if she went to school and quite dreadful if she went home. Ultimately, she would have to face this hurdle on another day, as she had many more school years ahead. From there, I readjusted the goal of her being there. I shifted my thinking from her going to school for two lessons as agreed, to her just becoming more comfortable being at school. It wasn't about getting hooked by her negative emotions: rather, it was about sitting with discomfort and finding a way to get into the classroom.

So I made the suggestion for her to go into the classroom for ten minutes. That was it. I told her I would wait in the car park and when she returned ten minutes later I would drive her home. It was a small enough commitment for her to agree. I can happily say that the next day she went to school for the full afternoon. On that first day, her anxiety was too high to see that as an option. Fortunately, she was self-aware enough to realise that she could manage a smaller goal.

That old mantra of 'never making a major decision when you are emotional' has served me well, time and time again, and there is solid research to back this up. In the *Journal of Neuroscience* (2016), scientists at the University of Pittsburgh demonstrated that when there is anxiety, the part of our brain that is essential for making good decisions is disengaged. Anxiety tends to direct our behaviour towards what feels like the safest option, rather than the best option for the long term.

The key is to manage with and through our anxiety. To know ourselves well enough so that we can manage ourselves well, despite the discomfort we are feeling. Self-awareness requires thinking and processing time. We always have more time than we think we do and it's important to recognise this and use it. Even just a few precious seconds can give us time to think through our options: Who do I need to be right now? How do I need to respond?

Values and character strengths

Values are the things that are important to us. They shape what we do and the decisions we make. Values are our heart's deepest desires for the way we want to interact with and relate to the world, other people and ourselves. They make up an important part of our identity. Difficulty directly challenges our values, and this can easily arouse strong emotions.

Values are absolutely essential to the foundation of who we are. The main benefit of knowing our values is that we gain tremendous clarity and focus. Values are priorities that tell us how to spend our time. If we don't consciously use our priorities and values to stick to a clear and consistent direction, then we will naturally drift off course and waste precious time.

We start to understand our values by looking at what is truly important to us: family, partner/marriage, parenting, friends/social life, work/career, education/training, sport and recreation, physical self-care (diet, exercise and sleep), community, spirituality. It's important to identify your top value. You are unlikely to have all of your values met in any one situation, so you need to rank them in order of priority and align them to your future self. My early focus was on my career only. I didn't have children and parenting was not a value on my radar. Some years later that changed and I became a mum. I shifted the value of my work, which is still a very important focus, to make room for being a parent. If I hadn't changed my values, my true potential of being a parent would have remained untapped.

Self-Awareness in Action
Values and Goals Exercise (give yourself plenty of time to do this exercise!)

Step 1: Determine what is important to you
What is truly important to you? In the following areas of your life, when you are being your best self, list all the values you can think of:
- Self-care, health (mind and body)
- Family, parenting
- Partner/marriage
- Friends/social life
- Career/work
- Spirituality
- Community

Step 2: Prioritise your values
From your list of values, highlight those that feel the most important. Think about how they guide how you behave to be your best self. It is important to narrow down what you want to focus on.

Step 3: Trimming down the list
See if you can narrow each values list to around ten for each area.

Step 4: Values alignment
Ask yourself the following questions:
- What do I need to do to live out these values more fully?
- How can they help me to show up?
- How can they help me navigate challenges and make decisions?

Step 5: Goals alignment
Take some time to write out your goals list in your Learning Journal. Take a look at your current value set and see if they will actually get you there.

Ask yourself: are my current values aligned with the goals I wish to achieve? If not, what values do I need to adjust, incorporate and prioritise?

If you keep living by your current values, then you can expect to get similar results to what you're already getting. But if there are parts of you that are not really satisfied with where you are at, the one and only way that you will get there is by shifting your values to align with your goals.

Once you have your updated values list, make them known to yourself. Check in with them daily. Carry them proudly and use them as your guides. Continue to reassess your values to ensure that they align best with the goals that you're trying to achieve.

Values are at play even when we don't realise, as I came to learn in Turkey in 1990. Women typically didn't walk around alone in Istanbul, especially at night, but as two 21-year-old girls, my travelling companion Dorotea and I felt like seasoned travellers. After all, we'd been on the road for many months. On this one particular evening, we had just finished dinner and were walking home, down a very dark street. It was about 9 pm. I was pretty attuned and alert. Five men appeared out of the darkness and began walking with us. In silence. Not one word was exchanged. It was surreal. My mind was racing. I was on high alert.

The next thing I heard was a scuffling, shuffling and gagging sound. Dorotea was on the ground squirming as the men held her down. She was gagging. I was frightened. Alone. Watching. I knew I could run. I could get away and save myself. But I also knew I had a choice. Save myself, or stay in this terrifying space and see if I could help my friend. I had a choice. In that split second I chose to stay. Moments later, a car emerged from a nearby laneway. On instinct, I raced over to the car, yelling at them to stop, hitting my hand on the bonnet of the car. Unbelievably, the driver wound up his window, turned off his lights and accelerated off. I was stunned. He was not willing to help. I looked back at my friend. Incredibly, the men had fled. The interruption from the car was enough to scare the men off. I helped Dorotea up from the ground and pretty much carried her home. Despite being badly bruised and shaken, no serious damage was done.

The story is about our values in stress and how they play out. For me personally it was a values turning point. I had unacknowledged values coming to the fore. The truth is, we don't really know how we're going to react under stress until tested. When we behave effectively our values get utilised – we don't live with the regret of the 'what ifs'. I learned how important people are to me. I had to put somebody else's needs before my own. This came at a point in my life when I was very selfish and definitely very reckless. The risk in me staying to help was that the men could turn on me, but I was willing to take it because without me Dorotea, alone, was in extreme danger. I later came to realise that maybe I wasn't as selfish as I thought. That night in Istanbul taught me more about who I really am.

Given that challenge makes us behave differently, it may come as no surprise that not all of our behaviours or responses can be predicted. When we go into survival mode, we can shift gears completely and become like someone else. What helps us in those moments of struggle are our values. When we know ourselves, our values become the signposts that guide us through. The more clearly we know them, the better we will handle ourselves in future stressful times. In Istanbul, I valued my friend and our friendship. I cared. I valued her safety. That became so clear to me in a split second. When you reflect on your own life, you will likely have had some clues, through your previous responses to stressful situations, to what is truly important to you. Below is a reflection exercise to see if you can uncover some of those values.

> ### ✎ Self-Awareness in Action
> Take some time out to capture in your Learning Journal your responses to the following questions:
> 1. Think back over a stressful event that you handled well. What did you do? How did you react?
> 2. Name the strengths and skills you used to cope effectively.
> 3. What were the values at play that guided you to do what you did?
> 4. After looking at your responses to the above questions, how confident do you feel about your own ability to handle future challenges? Do they help you to feel more hopeful about the future and your ability to cope well?

A part of knowing yourself is knowing what you are good at. Consulting firm Gallup did a meta-analysis of 2,708,538 employees and almost 112,312 business units in 2020 and found that people who have the opportunity to focus on their strengths every day are six times more likely to be engaged in their jobs and over three times more likely to report having an excellent life in general (Harter et al., 2020). As I often ask my clients: do you know why people want you in the room? You need to know what your unique value-add qualities and competencies are that make you indispensable. These are your strengths.

Character strengths are the positive parts of your personality that impact how you think, feel and behave. They lead to positive emotions and relationships, greater vitality, and meaningful life activities. And they help us in times of difficulty. When we identify and use our strengths, we flourish. Knowing and applying our highest character strengths helps us to be our best selves.

Focusing on strengthening a weakness is unlikely to create more value. I coach people to work on strengthening their strengths. Transforming something strong into something superb takes just as much effort but provides many more opportunities. But which strength to focus on? First you need to identify your strengths.

✎ Self-Awareness in Action

Take some time out in your Learning Journal to list your strengths. If you find this is a struggle, go find out what they are!
- You can start by asking people around you what they see as your strengths. Notice if they're not saying something that you think that they should.

Find out your character strengths:
- You can do a free character strengths assessment at www.viacharacter.org/survey/account/register
- Or you might like to try the Clifton Strengths Assessment (also free) at www.gallup.com/cliftonstrengths
- For a fee, you can receive the full report.

Once you have done this, answer these questions in your journal:
1. In which parts of your daily life can you incorporate your strengths more?
2. How might you use your strengths in the current challenges you are facing?

Scripts and self-efficacy

Who are we but the stories we tell ourselves,
about ourselves, and believe?
—Scott Turow, *Ordinary Heroes*

How you think about yourself and how you talk to yourself makes all the difference. Internal scripts are packages of expectations we put on ourselves and others about what people will do in given situations. They serve us because they organise our memories. Like an actor learning a script, they become habitual, but a static script doesn't serve us well over time. We need to continually question them to make sure that the way they once served us still holds true.

Sam was a confident happy little girl until she was 11 years old. That's when the bullying started. To survive, she internalised and did her own problem-solving. Eventually, she told her parents and it felt good to share. The school's solution was to ask Sam to share her experience with the whole class. In that moment, Sam denied everything. She wanted to be accepted. Sam learned not to trust or share her problems with others – it was safer that way. She kept all difficult tasks to herself. Fast forward 30 years, and we now have a CEO who doesn't share her day-to-day problems, preferring to solve things by herself. She does not delegate easily. Fear of judgement hasn't magically disappeared; neither has the need to be accepted. Sam still struggles to speak up. Unfortunately, this script carried into all aspects of her life. It became a behaviour choice and a well-versed script. Going back to the germination of this script helped pull it from Sam's non-conscious part of her brain up into the conscious part. She was able to look at it and question its usefulness.

Our beliefs lead to our thoughts, which lead to our behaviours.

All of us have different perspectives and experiences. Over time these perspectives solidify and typically sink below the water line until we are no longer conscious of their origin. We owe it to ourselves to dive below the water line. To become more self-aware of the thoughts, feelings and beliefs inside us (often held non-consciously) and how they got there. When we pull those stories up for air and examine them, we can recalibrate them to reflect who we are now and who we need to be. We need to hold onto our life scripts lightly and be prepared to review and redraft.

> ### ✏ Self-Awareness in Action
> When you say the following:
> - I always ...
> - I never ...
> - I should ...
>
> What do you say to yourself?
> Write it down in your Learning Journal.

Our internal scripts colour how we believe in our own abilities – our self-efficacy. Albert Bandura described our beliefs as the things that determine how people think, behave and feel. This means that how you feel about yourself can play a role in whether or not you successfully achieve your goals in life. Self-efficacy, according to Bandura, plays a major role in how we perceive and respond to situations. The role of your self-efficacy in who you are today is absolutely vital and plays a major role in how your goals, tasks and challenges are approached.

Research by Tuckman (1990), found that people who believed more in themselves (high believers) performed beyond their own expectations and the performance of low believers fell short of their own expectations. In other words, our belief in our own ability is an important mediator between self-expectations and actual fulfilment of our purpose. If you have low self-efficacy you might avoid challenging tasks, believing they are beyond your control or capability. A negative internal script will run. Self-confidence in your own abilities is harder to maintain. On the other hand, if you have strong self-efficacy you tend to view challenging problems as simply another task to be mastered. This can fuel a deeper interest in activities so you can form a stronger sense of commitment. It helps you bounce back from disappointments and setbacks.

> ### ✎ Self-Awareness in Action
> Self-efficacy is a skill that you can build and develop using some of the following strategies:
> - Work on setting stretch goals that are achievable but not necessarily easy. They will take work and perseverance, but you will emerge with a stronger belief in your own abilities once you achieve them.
> - Identify somebody who is doing well in a particular area and model yourself against them. Using the observations that you make of them, incorporate their behaviours into what you do. Seeing their success can increase your belief in your ability to do the same.
> - Hearing positive feedback from others can help improve your sense of self-efficacy. Seek out positive affirmations from people you rate highly. Try to avoid asking for feedback from people who you know are more likely to have a negative or critical view of your performance. Positive social feedback can be helpful for strengthening your already existing sense of self-efficacy.
> - Pay attention to your thoughts and emotions. Look for ways to manage them if they are getting in the way of what you want to accomplish. For example, look for ways to ease your stress levels to help make you feel more confident in your capabilities.

'Everyone has a story, including you. Use yours for fuel and reinvention.'

—Trina Pitcher

Anchor Self – Self-Awareness

Take some time out to conduct your Self-Awareness DIY Assessment.

Give yourself a score out of 10, where 10 is true all of the time and 1 is never true.

Self-Awareness	1–10
I have an excellent understanding of my strengths	
I have a clear sense of how I am feeling throughout the day	
I have an excellent understanding of my weaknesses	
I know when one of my 'hot buttons' is being pressed	
I manage myself well at all times	
I have a clear understanding of my values	
I know why I think and behave the way I do	
I welcome feedback from others	
Self-Awareness TOTAL	

When you have added up your score, out of a total of 80, colour in your Self-Awareness Anchor score on the circumplex. Use the scoring key as your guide. As you progress through this book, you can return to this assessment and continue to colour in the various Anchors to build your Anchor profile.*

---

* At the end of the book, your individual Anchor scores can be translated across to form your Anchor Self-profile.

SELF-AWARENESS

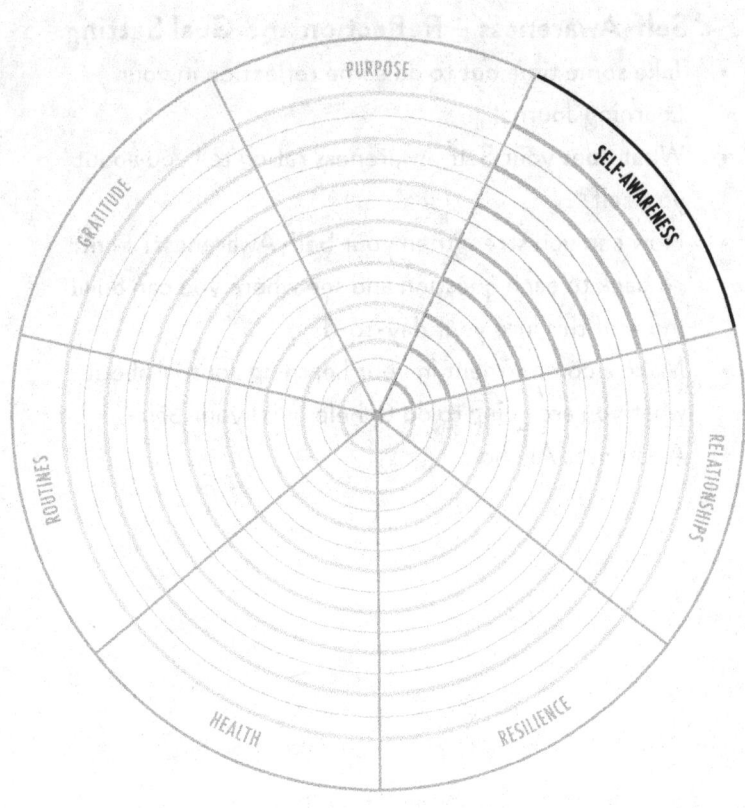

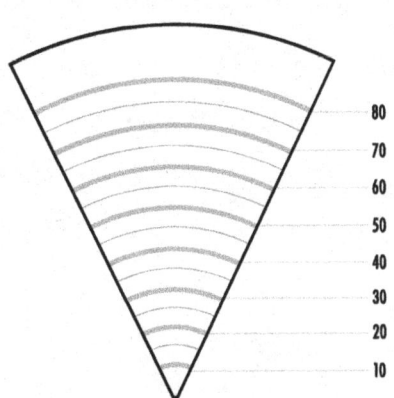

Scoring Key

> ### ✏️ Self-Awareness – Reflection and Goal Setting
> - Take some time out to do some reflection in your Learning Journal.
> - What does your Self-Awareness rating tell you about yourself?
> - How can you strengthen your Self-Awareness? Hint: go back to each question and see where you can build more of this into your day-to-day.
> - Make a commitment in your Learning Journal about what you are going to do to help build your Self-Awareness Anchor.

6

Purpose

When you find your why, you don't hit snooze no more!
You find a way to make it happen!
—Eric Thomas

I love this quote. Eric Thomas was a high-school dropout, brought up by his single mum in Detroit. In his early years he faced incredible challenges that saw him homeless. After the support and guidance of a preacher he managed to turn his life around and focus on what matters. Since then, he has inspired many others to do the same.

Why is Purpose important?

Ultimately, man should not ask what the meaning of his life is, but rather must recognize that it is he who is asked. In a word, each man is questioned by life; and he can only answer to life by answering for his own life; to life he can only respond by being responsible.
—Victor Frankl

This classic quote, in Frankl's *Man's Search For Meaning*, points to our personal responsibility to search for our unique meaning and purpose. Very few of us actually spend time thinking about ourselves. We don't naturally think about why we are on this planet and where we are going.

Incredibly, the majority of people don't even plan their own future. Or, if they do, it is done very loosely. Living with purpose gives you a focus on the things that matter most to you and where you add value. I am great at doing the dishes, but my time would be better spent getting the roast in the oven. Through your purpose, you will find a sense of contribution and accomplishment and get a sense of fulfilment from it. It's your north star.

I ask many of my clients to think about what they want their lives to be like ten years from now. When people don't plan ahead it indicates to me that they don't have purpose. Many of us only think within our current role until we are ready for the next move. We are typically raised to think of others and do for others: for our boss, for our kids, for our teams. We need to climb up to the balcony for a global, distant view of our lives so we can plan the future. Purpose supports our decision-making and keeps us on track.

Some years ago, I was at a 'check-in' meeting with my client, a CEO, and her boss, who just so happened to be a rabbi! During the meeting, the rabbi told us something that I have never forgotten, and it has made a huge impact on my life. He told us that God has given each and every one of us three things. The first thing God gave us was a purpose. A purpose for being on this planet. To elaborate, the rabbi said that it is our duty and responsibility to find out what our unique purpose is. The second thing God gave us was all the skills and abilities we need to fulfil our purpose. But, he said, the third thing that God gave us was only a limited time in which to fulfil that purpose. After he finished telling us this, the room fell silent. I knew exactly what he was talking about, I'd just never heard it said so succinctly. Over the years I have repeated this story many times and I hope it resonates with you as much as it did me.

For years I have observed those around me who know their Purpose. These purpose-driven people have an energy about them, a light in their eyes, and they seem to survive setbacks much better than others around them. They are driven and have a reason to get out of bed in the morning. They seem to know their 'Why'. I've also noticed that having a life purpose is perhaps more important than the purpose itself.

Every one of us has our own unique purpose – whether it is known to its owner is a completely different matter. And as the rabbi mused in his final point to us, it is our duty alone to find out what it is, so that we may fulfil it.

If I reflect on all my clients over the past 20 years, those who truly flourished had three things in common. Firstly, they all chose to live a life with purpose, on purpose. They had something meaningful to drive their lives. Second, their behaviours and choices were fuelled, guided and underpinned by their values. And third, they each had bucketloads of courage. By aligning purpose, values and courage they got on with fulfilling their goals.

Perhaps you already notice others around you seem to have more meaning, energy and engagement in their lives. They are more deliberate in how they spend their time. Their relationships look great, their jobs are rewarding and their sense of direction compels them to hop out of bed each morning with a spring in their step. Both my brothers have been like that for years. They get a lot done and are very good at taking deliberate time out to look after themselves in order to keep on keeping on. They both lead fulfilling lives and have created significant contributions outside themselves. What I eventually came to realise was that they, as with all my successful clients, have purpose, commitment and direction.

In my younger years I was curious and kind of envious because I didn't feel like I knew my purpose. So began my research on how to work it out, in the hope that I might discover mine along the way. Fast-forward some 25-odd years and I can now say that I have a very clearly articulated purpose and have helped many people find and articulate theirs. What has also become apparent to me is that when you are clear on your purpose, others around you will know what you stand for too.

What happens when we don't have a clear purpose?

Feeling purposeless can lead to losing your sense of identity. You might find yourself looking to others to make your decisions: to tell you what's right, what you should or shouldn't be doing. If you feel this way, this might be the first time you question why, or where the feeling is coming from.

Here are a few indicators that may give you clues that you're not living out your purpose:

- When your work feels like a tick-box exercise to pay the bills and put food on the table, and the real joy happens outside the workplace. You may even have some good friends at work, but you don't have energy or enthusiasm to be there. Being there drains your energy. The work itself isn't satisfying and doesn't engage you.
- Other times you may feel stuck or trapped with where you are in your life or work. This is a horrible feeling exacerbated by a feeling of helplessness, of not knowing how to get out of feeling that way. You may find that you ruminate, you relive memories of the past or have goals for the future, but don't have the steps to resolve to move forward. It becomes dreadfully frustrating and thoroughly demoralising.
- Closely linked to this is when you feel unrewarded by what you do, that the things in your life don't bring you joy, fulfilment or satisfaction. It's like there is no colour in your world. You may find that your job doesn't utilise your skills or interests, your relationships are unrewarding and unfulfilling, and your activities don't give you pleasure or joy. Rather, they feel boring and tedious.
- When you are not managing your time deliberately or well you tend not to do what you're meant to be doing, or you are not where you're meant to be. The internal script for this has a lot of 'shoulds' in it, which comes from the external pressures of others and their expectations rather than through your own internal decision-making. You lack a sense of urgency and may even feel guilty about that too.

- You may also feel that you have nothing to look forward to or work towards. You don't have life goals. This comes with a sense of aimlessness and a lack of sense of progression.

If you feel any or all of the above, then it is likely that you will gain tremendous benefit from tethering yourself to the Purpose Anchor and being able to articulate yours. The good news is while there's no one pathway for discovering your purpose, there are many ways you can gain deeper insight into yourself, and a better perspective on what it is that you have to offer the world.

What the research says

He who has a why can endure any how.
—Friedrich Nietzsche

Most people don't just wake up one day and suddenly know their purpose. It takes time, effort and introspection. According to Arruda et al. (2013), 'If you want to be successful, you need to think of yourself as a personal brand.' They says a personal purpose statement is a critical piece of your brand because it helps you stay focused and is, after all, our ultimate guide. Kashdan and McKnight (2009) describe our purpose as a central, self-organising life aim that stimulates goals. And according to Victor Strecher (2016), having a purpose correlates highly with psychological wellness and even with markers of physical health and longevity. He also found that people with a purpose had less depressive symptoms and greater blood flow into the reward centre of their brains (ventral striatum). Other studies have found that students try harder when they consider education important for their careers. And others found that those who have a strong sense of meaning in their lives are twice as likely to live longer and lessen the risk of heart conditions.

We all need to focus on making ours the best life possible and check ourselves regularly to ensure we don't get hooked on unhelpful habits embedded in our early years. If what you have read already isn't compelling enough, living in line with your purpose insures you from living a life of regret. In 1979 Erma Bombeck, an American humorist, was asked if she had her life over, would she change anything. This was her response:

> When my child kissed me impetuously, I would never have said, 'Later. Now, go get washed up for dinner.' There would have been more I love yous … more I'm sorrys … more I'm listenings … but mostly, given another shot at life, I would seize every minute of it … look at it and really see it … try it on … live it … exhaust it … and never give that minute back until there was nothing left of it.

According to a survey conducted by Deloitte:

> In the workplace employees who feel a sense of purpose in their work tend to be happier, healthier and more productive. Businesses who are clear on their purpose have been found to be more enjoyable places to work and more financially successful. 91% of workers who say their company has a strong sense of purpose also report a history of strong financial performance. A culture of purpose in an organisation guides behaviour, influences strategy, transcends leaders – and endures.
> —Punit Renjen, Deloitte Global CEO

Purpose Toolkit
Topics covered:
- understanding purpose
- an organisation's purpose
- macro- and micro-purpose
- courage
- creating your purpose statement.

Understanding Purpose

I ask all my clients, in the early stages of working with them, what they do and why they do it. What I am searching for is not only how their role fits in to the organisation but also whether what they do resonates with them as a person. Does their role align with and feed into who they want to be in life? This also gives me an idea of how much they know about themselves.

Let me give you an example about a client who worked in an aluminium factory. The factory was a commercial organisation, so profit was its main objective. His role was in sales and distribution but his focus, and what the company rewarded him for, were the numbers and the dollars made or saved. When I asked him to tell me a little more, he said something along the lines of, 'I have to balance spreadsheets and manage company spend versus incoming.' When I asked him why he did that, he looked at me rather dumbfounded and gave me a stock-standard answer, 'Well, that's my job.' Businesses inherently function by employing people to 'do their jobs'. But, as we all know, there are many ways to approach your job. There are those who just treat their job as a tick-box exercise, so that they can get home and live their lives. And there are those who treat their job as a vocation that forms a large part of their life fulfilment.

We also had a conversation around the sort of person he was. He wanted, in his life, to be someone who was helpful and supportive of others – his purpose. As the conversation went on and when we incorporated his purpose in his role, the penny started to drop. It turned out that he was really ensuring that roofs were being effectively, timely and economically put on people's houses so they could sleep safely at night. Quality had to be good enough so that it would withstand the weather and the price had to be reasonable enough so the customer could afford it. Oh, and the company needed to make a profit. When seen in this light, the role was no longer numbers on a spreadsheet; rather, it was connected to the world in which we live. For the first time in my client's mind, his job connected to his purpose.

When I worked at a consulting firm, I had the opportunity to work for a tobacco company. My role was to increase performance across their senior leadership group. On the one hand, it appeared to involve all the things I loved doing – helping people be better, coaching, running workshops, assessments and more. But there was one big problem that rendered the role untenable for me. In my heart of hearts, I could not bring myself to work for a company where my purpose was so far out of alignment. This company was responsible for damaging people's lives. I clearly wasn't. If I had taken this role, it would have gone against who and what I stand for and dishonoured who I am as a person. When we are clear on our values and purpose, we can identify where our edge is – what's in and what's out. It makes saying 'No' much easier.

> ### ✎ Purpose in Action
> Take some time out to answer the following questions. Write the answers down in your Learning Journal.
>
> Name a role that you have done/or you are doing that does not feel right for you:
> - What was/is the purpose of this organisation/team and how did/does your role fit in?
> - In what way were/are you unsatisfied?
> - What could have made the difference for you? Is there something that could have made it more appealing?
> - Was/is there a mismatch between your own and the organisation's purpose?
> - Which of your own values did/does it clash with? (Please name them.)

An organisation's purpose

If you work, your work for an organisation will have a purpose – something it hopes to achieve. It is the 'what' and the 'why' of an organisation's work and is the reason the organisation exists. All of its activities should contribute to achieving that purpose in some way. In terms of purpose, there are essentially two categories of organisation. The first, a commercial organisation, essentially exists to generate a profit. The owner may decide to keep or share the profit. The second, a non-commercial organisation, will provide some sort of service to the community. It is not established for the purpose of earning a profit. Some examples of not-for-profit (NFP) organisations include: Red Cross, World Health Organization, arts, civic, cultural, education, and health and human services, such as schools, community centres, galleries and hospitals. Because purpose goes to the heart of a NFP's identity, any changes to it are often the product of a collaborative process involving considerable thought and debate.

All of the above have one thing in common. They all serve a purpose. Here are a few examples:

- Woolworths Group: We create better experiences together that better people's lives.
- Medibank Private: Better health for better lives.
- Ramsay Health Care: People caring for people.
- AGL Energy: Helping to shape a sustainable energy future for Australia.
- Coca Cola: To refresh the world ... To inspire moments of optimism and happiness ... To create value and make a difference.
- Google: To organise the world's information and make it universally accessible and useful.
- TED: To spread ideas.
- RSPCA Australia: To prevent cruelty to animals by actively promoting their care and protection.

- Opera Australia: To present opera that excites audiences and sustains and develops the art form.
- Vision Australia: To support people who are blind or have low vision to live the life they choose.

Macro- and micro-purpose

We each have an overarching purpose that I call a macro-purpose. It's our unique fingerprint for our life. Our macro-purpose allows us to zoom out and look at the big picture view of who we are. In that space, we are not concerned with the details of how things are to be done, but instead our broad 'Why'.

Usually we have several different roles in life, each with different requirements – a parent, a worker, a friend, a community member. Each role naturally needs us to do different things and has its own unique purpose – something I call a micro-purpose. To be effective in life, you will have around seven or so micro-purposes. They feed into and enable us to fulfil our macro-purpose. They take our 'Why' and zoom into the detail. When our micro-purposes are well defined and in line with our roles, we are setting ourselves up to manage well both in them and across them.

My macro-purpose is to help others be more equipped to live and lead better lives. My micro-purpose as a mum is to help my kids to be empowered to be independent and good decision-makers, to care for themselves and others. For me, I need to be fit, healthy, present, switched on and a good role model. I also need to surround myself with great friends and great relationships, showing them that I care for myself and for others. Further, that I can get back up and keep going even when life is hard. It means being someone who is loving and supportive and contributing to the planet that I live on.

In terms of my work, my micro-purpose is to empower people to find their courage to live great lives and navigate through difficulty. I achieve this in my coaching, counselling, leadership development and speaking engagements. Even writing this book helps me fulfil that micro-purpose. But for many years I didn't realise how all the various parts of me and my roles meshed together. I didn't have the thread until I discovered micro-purposes.

Your macro-purpose statement can be inspired by others but it must resonate with your own needs. Here are a few purpose statements to help you refine yours:

- To live a life of honesty, integrity and unconditional love.
- To help new leaders make sound and effective decisions.
- To inspire change through teaching.
- To support and elevate those around me.
- To leave the world a better place than I found it.
- Elon Musk: To do useful things that work, make people's lives better and make the future better.
- Oprah Winfrey: To be a teacher. And to be known for inspiring my students to be more than they thought they could be.
- Sir Richard Branson: To have fun in [my] journey through life and learn from [my] mistakes.

Courage

To live your purpose, as with all the 7 Anchors, you need courage. The courage to say 'No' and the courage to say 'Yes', and the ability to differentiate the impact of those decisions. You will need the courage to live in line with your values. None of this is easy. When you feel you are swimming against the tide, it can take a bucketload of courage to keep moving in that direction. But when you use your values as your guide to act in line with your purpose you will find strength to overcome challenges. The word courage comes from the Latin route 'cor', meaning heart. Courage is about acting from your heart despite the fear and possible repercussions. Courageous behaviour is guided by knowing who you are and what you stand for.

Late last year I was asked to deliver a brand-new five-day online training program on my own for the first time. It is a complicated program, with lots of moving parts, designed to have two facilitators working in tandem, along with an assistant to manage the tricky online logistics. As a facilitator, the preparation is considerable. I only had three weeks to prepare for and run the workshop.

I mulled over it for days and decided to decline the offer. I knew in my heart it wasn't for me. What sat behind that decision was reminding myself of who I'm trying to be and the values I uphold. To prepare for the workshop would have meant working most evenings and across my weekends, as I was fully booked during the day with other work. This would have impacted time with the kids and my ability to be a mum. There would be no downtime over those weeks if I was to deliver a high-quality product. It wasn't an easy decision and I don't like saying no. But to say yes would have been worse. It would have compromised who I am as a person, and I'm not willing to do that for myself, for my kids or my clients.

Creating your purpose statement

Your macro-purpose statement should be front and centre of who you are. It can give you focus and help keep you motivated to reach your goals. When you are clear about your purpose, others around you shouldn't have to search for it. A good purpose statement will help drive your work to deliver on your goals, even when things are really tough.

To find your purpose, look at your strengths. If you don't know what they are, ask people around you what they've noticed you are really good at. It may surprise you that you have very specific gifts and strengths. Perhaps you're a gifted writer or a tremendous speaker or influencer. Maybe you are an excellent problem-solver or have great skill at taking in large amounts of information, analysing it or simplifying it. You might be great at organising people and getting things done. Your macro-purpose often combines the things you're already good at with your passions.

The things we are good at often align with our purpose. Better still, we usually enjoy doing them. Finding your passions involves reflecting your interests across all parts of your life. What do you really love doing?

Business, economics, helping others, taking care of animals, the planet, food, the arts, activism and so on. If you had no restrictions what would you love to do? Knowing your passions is a great place to start looking for purpose. You also need to look outward. Who are the people in your life that you impact? What can they expect from you? How can they expect you to deliver it? When you get to use both your strengths and passions, life feels amazing. That's when you hear people say – I don't feel like I work, because I love what I do and it's such a pleasure to do it.

✎ Purpose in Action

Take some time out now to identify your macro-purpose. Complete the following in your Learning Journal:
- Name your five or six strengths.
- Name your passions and strong interests.

Commonly known purposes in life typically fall within these or a combination of these categories:
- success/career success
- feeling loved
- having a positive impact on others
- inspiring others
- home and family
- being happy
- living authentically
- fortune
- being creatively expressive
- fostering connections
- living mindfully
- achieving life balance
- protecting the environment
- raising successful kids
- living with joy/happiness

- leaving a legacy
- making others happy
- teaching/educating.

Which of these resonate with you? Write them down.

This is about focusing your life on what matters most. It defines boundaries that will help keep you focused.

But it's not just about yourself. Keep others in mind. This is also about the people you want to impact.

Have a go at defining your macro-purpose statement. Keep it short. You want this to be something you can sum up in a single sentence.

My macro-purpose is to _____, so that (target audience) will _____. From here, create seven micro-purpose statements for your differing roles.

Once you've written your purpose statements be sure to share them with others. Eventually they will 'leak' out of you in all that you do.

*'Owning our story can
be hard but not nearly as
difficult as spending our
lives running from it.'*

—Brené Brown

Anchor Self – Purpose

Take some time out to conduct your Purpose DIY Assessment.

Give yourself a score out of 10, where 10 is true all of the time and 1 is never true.

Purpose	1–10
I understand my purpose in life	
In my day to day, I know what gives meaning to my life	
My decisions about what I do are always worthwhile	
People who I work closely with know my life's purpose	
I feel motivated to make the most of every day	
I make decisions so that I do not live with regret	
I have the courage to live out my life's purpose	
I have values and beliefs that help me know who I am	
Purpose TOTAL	

When you have added up your score, out of a total of 80, colour in your Purpose Anchor score on the circumplex. Use the Scoring Key as your guide. As you progress through this book, you can return to your assessment and continue to colour in the various Anchors.*

---

* At the end of the book, your individual Anchor scores can be translated across to form your Anchor Self-profile.

PURPOSE

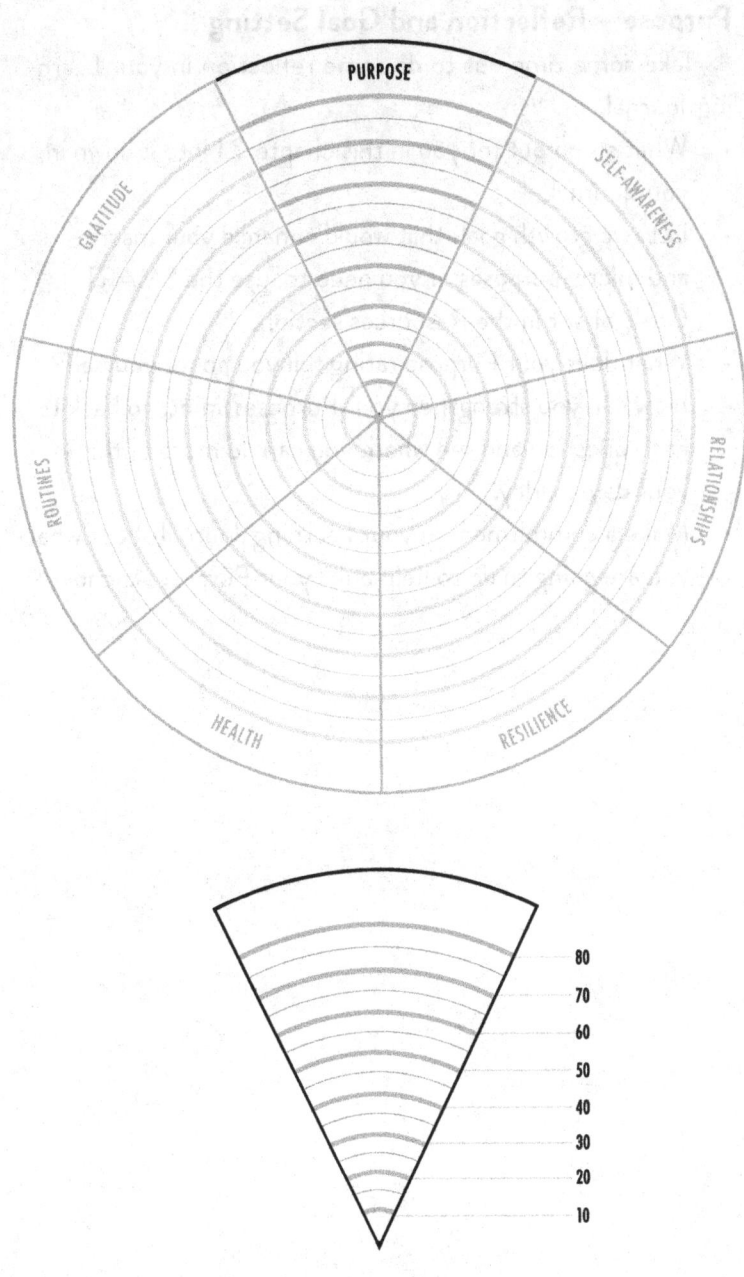

Scoring Key

Purpose – Reflection and Goal Setting

✎ Take some time out to do some reflection in your Learning Journal.
- What stood out for you in this chapter? Note it down in your journal.
- List two growth goals that would enhance your macro- and micro-purposes. If you need to, use the SMART Goals Sheet in the Resources section.
- What does your Purpose rating tell you about yourself?
- How can you strengthen your Purpose? Hint: go back to each question and see where you can do more of this in your day-to-day.
- Make a commitment in your Learning Journal about what you are going to do to help build your Purpose Anchor.

7

Relationships

When we think about relationships, it's easy to overlook our relationship with ourselves. This is the relationship that builds the foundation for how well we relate to others. All relationships are important. We all have different interpersonal needs, and when we learn how to build quality relationships in all areas of our lives, we realise that relationship difficulties can occupy a large part of life's difficulties. This makes the Relationships Anchor fundamental for you to live a great life.

Why are Relationships important?

When we unpack this question, we realise just how many parts of our lives are touched by relationships. In my work as a coach, all my clients want to be better, in some shape or form. But what does being better involve? A big predictor of their success is reflected in their relationships. The clients who manage their 'inner worlds' tend to function a lot better. They understand and know themselves well enough to have a realistic and positive relationship with themselves. They have great support networks and interests outside of work and just enough friends and family to be supportive but not burdensome. At work they are well networked and have people around them who believe in them. They are seen as valuable and good to work with and for. Relationships are all about quality not just quantity. You can build good-quality relationships when you have the ability to adjust your sails and manage the complexities that inevitably come up. This doesn't just automatically happen – it takes work, commitment and refinement – but the rewards are spectacular.

There is a quote attributed most often to motivational speaker Jim Rohn, 'You're the average of the five people you spend the most time with.' Or perhaps, 'Show me your friends and I'll show you your future.' The idea is to make sure you are spending time with people who support what you want for your own life. It's compelling. It's provocative. It requires self-awareness. Surround yourself with people who have your best interest in mind.

> ### ✎ Relationships in Action
> Take some time out in your Learning Journal to audit the people around you.
> 1. How much time do you spend with them? (Pick your top five, and continue on.)
> 2. How would you describe them, what qualities and values do they demonstrate – the good and the bad?
> 3. Do they have your best interests at heart – seriously, do they?
> 4. Do they want to see you succeed?
> 5. Do they support your decisions of self-improvement?
> 6. Are they there in the bad times as well as the good?

Asking for help

As with any big project, I went through a number of phases and stages while writing this book. Along the way, three notable and fairly predictable obstacles emerged. In the beginning I was filled with momentum and energy and churned through the writing easily and happily. But then, I went through periods of lost focus, became unproductive and fell behind schedule. I even questioned why I was writing it. I'd find any excuse to do something else: water the garden, go for a run, pat the dog, make a coffee, eat, fold clothes, pat the dog again. I was doing anything but the writing. And I was acutely aware that this was procrastination. The third phase began at the point of reflection, when I realised that this book would not happen unless I tapped into my reason for writing it.

PHASE I	PHASE II	PHASE III

Enthusiasm to task → an event or distraction from task → Reflection to re-engagement or disengagement to task (productivity) → (low or no productivity) → (re-engagement to productivity, or exit from)

I agreed on a writing schedule and submission dates with my writing coach. Productivity kicked in again. But then things changed. My first submission was late. Other stuff was happening in my life that took me off task. The next submission was also late. I take pride in keeping commitments and missing two deadlines made me feel dreadful. I felt the full weight of disappointing my coach and not keeping to the schedule. I had let both of us down. When I spoke to him about it, I told him honestly that I felt things weren't going well, that I was finding it tough and was feeling restless and unable to focus. My writing just didn't have the same flow that it did when I wrote the first few chapters. Having never written a book before, the whole journey and process was an unknown. He asked me what I needed to do to help myself.

With the time and space to reflect, I realised I needed to tap in to the 7 Anchor Model to see what I could do to lift myself up. We laughed as I realised that creating and writing about the 7 Anchor Model didn't absolve me from needing it. I would need to regularly check in with my Anchors to keep me on track. It was wonderful to see that as soon as we talked about what was happening and could recognise what was needed, I did just that. The 7 Anchor Model laid out signposts for what I needed to do; it helped me rebalance. Just knowing what to do made me feel so much better. In that process, I reminded myself of the purpose of the book and why it needed to be written.

Life is slippery

We slip regularly. The important thing is that we know how to get back on track. Strong, open and honest relationships can, among other things, help fast-track this process of reflection and problem-solving. Being vulnerable, honest and authentic with my writing coach afforded me support, comfort and a way forward. That is a positive relationship. When things are tricky, when you lose focus, when you plateau and you want to help yourself in the best way possible way, your relationships are critical. It also allows you to do the very same for others.

Isolation

Whether for good or for bad, Covid exposed the vital importance of our relationships. My organisational clients had staff locked down alone in small apartments with no family. Isolation became a huge challenge to overcome. Several of my own clients were also living alone, but some managed considerably better than others. The differentiator, as I saw it, was the quality of their relationships. Those that had strong, open, trusting and loving relationships seemed to navigate through the bumpy times so much better than those who didn't. Even at arm's length it was a support structure. When we understand just how critical our relationships are, it reminds us to take care of them. To cultivate, nurture and feed them. Being mindful is the very first step.

✎ Relationships in Action

Take some time out to answer the following questions in your Learning Journal:

1. Do I share my difficulties with anyone, and if so who with?
2. Do they know about my current struggles and challenges, and if not, why not?
3. What stops me from opening up?
4. Who might I be able to open up to fully? (Please name them.)

> 5. If I had the chance to open up to someone right now, what would I share with them?
> 6. Does anyone share their struggles with me?
> 7. Could I be more receptive to allowing others to come and talk to me?
> 8. Which relationship(s) could I foster to allow for an open trusting dialogue?
>
> If the answer to 8 is 'no-one', you will find ways to be open to building new relationships later in this chapter.

When I was in my early twenties, I had been travelling for about eight months, having already travelled through England and Scotland among many other places. I was essentially alone but made great friends as I worked a variety of interesting jobs along the way. My trip was going brilliantly. I was 'living' while on holidays, but it was also getting hard, and not in the way I was expecting it to. I started to struggle with the 'goodbyes'. I found it extremely difficult to say goodbye to what felt like a revolving door of new-found besties (remember, I was only in my early twenties). So, when I arrived in Israel I decided to do a little personal social experiment.

The plan was to stop being outwardly social and not get close to anyone. I thought this might help protect me from the inevitable goodbyes. I found a job working in a local bar and rented a room in an apartment in Tel Aviv with a lovely Brazilian girl. Sticking to my plan, I worked nights and pottered about during the day. Alone. Before too long I started to feel unwell. I developed a knot in the pit of my stomach and a lump in my throat that followed me around all day. In the beginning I couldn't make sense of these uncomfortable feelings. My mood dropped and I started to lose my usual vibrant energy and happy self.

The 'unsociable experiment' was only in its third week, but it didn't take much to put two and two together. What I realised quite quickly was that I was lonely. What surprised me was that I was feeling it physically!

I immediately quit the experiment and made a concerted effort to go out and meet people and make connections, to be more open and make some new friends. I allowed myself once again to be my old friendly self. In the following days, the lump in my throat and the knot in the pit of my stomach faded away and my mood lifted. I realised in that crazy experiment that I'm someone who needs people, at least some of the time. I need close relationships, even if they don't last. That was a good 30 years ago, but it still holds true for me today. Thanks to the research of Will Schutz, PhD, I now know where it comes from.

What the research says

Back in 1952, during the Korean War, Schutz was recalled by the US Navy to do research on understanding and predicting how any given group of men would work together. He came up with a three-dimensional theory of interpersonal behaviour or needs. The theory implies that we all have the desire to express and receive needs for inclusion, control and affection, and that this varies in both amount and intensity from person to person. It is the variation in degree and magnitude that differentiates one person from another and impacts how and when we interact with others.

Understanding these needs gives us further insight into who we are, in terms of what motivates our behaviour and how much interaction we want with and from others. As with all motives, satisfying these needs motivates and energises us. Alternatively, we feel depleted of energy and demotivated when our interpersonal needs are either not met or demanded too heavily upon. I have had many clients who tell me how much they hate networking functions and how they find them exhausting. When they realise that their interpersonal need for inclusion is low they can understand what's going on for them, prepare for these events and build in some recovery time.

In the same way we have physiological needs described to us by Maslow's *Hierarchical Theory of Human Needs* (1943), we also have an inherent need for relationships. If you haven't come across it before, Abraham Maslow's theory argues that humans have a series of needs, some of which must be met before they can turn their attention toward others. Certain universal needs are the most pressing, while more 'acquired' emotions are of secondary importance. Knowing that relationships fulfil an inherent need of the human condition can help you understand your own interpersonal needs. When we use Schutz's perspective of inclusion, control and affection we can start to recognise that we all have different needs. This helped me understand why I became both mentally and physically depleted in my short unsocial experiment in Israel.

According to Pamela Valencia, a Solutions Consultant with CPP Professional Services: 'If your interpersonal needs are low, chances are that you don't feel a strong pull to be around others. Intellectual stimulation, activities you do alone, and privacy are probably more important to you. If your interpersonal needs fall more in the medium range, your interaction with others may sometimes be a source of satisfaction, but it will depend on with whom and the context of the situation. If your interpersonal needs are medium to high, then interaction with others will usually be a source of satisfaction for you (getting those interpersonal needs met), and you probably have regular contact with friends. People with medium high or high interpersonal needs prefer regular contact with a large group of friends, and at the high end may avoid situations that require working alone for long periods of time.'

When I think of who I am today, I feel like I have a rich and full life. I have a handful of extraordinarily close, trusting, authentic friends who both carry me and nourish me. I feel enabled and genuinely empowered by them to do whatever I want in life. My closest friends believe in me and I in them. I have their support and they have my back. They have seen me at my worst and stood by me when I have not had the capacity to think clearly or find a way forward. They have also celebrated my successes. They are helping fight through the struggles I face in life. They also know what I stand for.

My diverse friends (and colleagues) are scattered across the country. When I bring them together for birthdays or work catch-ups, we all get along and enjoy our time together. A single relationship is not the total answer, but together they come very close. Each of us have our edges and limitations, and we accept and understand that. We laugh together, we cry together, and we have a whole lot of fun together. Over the years I have worked very hard to choose my friends carefully. I know that I am very fortunate to have quality friendships. I understand that just like nutrition or fitness, it is something that benefits from deliberate focus.

Relationships Toolkit

Topics covered:
- your relationship with yourself
- the imposter phenomenon
- trust in yourself
- workplace relationships
- workplace conflict and difficult conversations
- trust at work
- networking
- building quality relationships.

Your Relationship with yourself

Your relationship with yourself is arguably the most important relationship in your life. We learn how to relate to ourselves from the key people in our lives: our parents, siblings, family, peers and other adults. As we grow up, the way we are treated by others, and the way we observe others treating themselves, influences how we care for ourselves. We learn what is good, and what is bad, what is pleasing and what is not.

We can't truly empathise with another person until we're able to identify and have compassion for our own feelings. The aim is a balance of healthy self-love. What this means is that I value myself. I care and look after myself to the best of my ability just like the legendary L'Oréal ad, 'Because I'm Worth It.' (As an aside, fascinatingly, although this was the phrasing used in their early ads, the current one is 'Because

You're Worth It'. Apparently, it was changed because women didn't feel comfortable saying 'I'm worth it'.) Caring for yourself involves being aware of and accepting your own limitations and needs. Listening to your inner voice and using it as a guide. The trick is choosing the right voice from the many shouting or whispering to you. The most dominant voice can be ruthless and downright nasty: 'You're such an idiot', 'You're a fool', 'Who the hell do you think you are?' or 'You don't belong here!'

Learning to pay less attention to the critical voice is crucial to building a good relationship with yourself. If your friend spoke to you like that, would you still be friends? Think about how you would speak to a small child who is learning a new skill. If you berate or shame them, they wouldn't really feel like trying again. If you show them encouragement, kindness, tolerance, they are more likely to explore, make mistakes and, ultimately, grow. My inner critic still talks to me, but it's nowhere near as dominant as it used to be. I am grateful that it tries to point out the risks that I may be about to face. In the past this voice may likely have served and saved me. What I choose to pay attention to now is the voice that speaks in line with my values and reminds me of who I am trying to be. It is the voice of encouragement; the one that tells me how important it is to look after myself.

By taking care of our ourselves, we are taking care of each other.

✎ Relationships in Action
Listen to and take note of how you speak to yourself across the day. Note in your Learning Journal what you say to yourself:
- when things are going well
- when things are going badly.

What do you think you could say differently when things are going badly? What words would you use to be kinder and more compassionate to yourself?

Only this morning I was working with a new client. Prior to our session she'd sent me an introductory email explaining that she felt lost and unhappy in her present role. She wanted to move from what felt like a static job but couldn't land on a specific problem. She'd say, 'Oh, there's nothing much to tell you. I'm just not happy at work.' She appeared very guarded, either avoiding questions or responding so generally that I was unable to determine the relevance. I had no tangible information to work with. Yet she was keen to keep going with the sessions. She wasn't deliberately trying to be difficult; she had simply never allowed herself time to think about her own wants, needs, likes, dislikes, or even who she was. She lacked any sort of curiosity about who she was. With no interest in, or compassion for, herself, she was unable to nourish herself and grow. This made it extremely difficult for her to connect with others in a meaningful way, leaving her isolated and alone.

Her first assumption was that her dissatisfaction with life was externally driven. She had tried (and failed) for promotion on several occasions, yet never sought feedback on her strengths and weaknesses. She told me that she had stopped asking questions of herself long ago. She felt no connection with any of her colleagues. Her 360 Survey revealed a lack of connection, poor self-awareness and poor communication. Communication with her boss was through emails because some years back they'd had a falling out. She was even pushing me away, and I was there to help. She said she wished things were different but had no idea how to change them.

If you are reading the Anchors in order, you would have already picked up that her Self-Awareness and Relationships Anchors needed a lot of work. Fortunately, I had managed to build enough trust over the course of our conversations that she was willing to try. I challenged her and neither she nor I walked away. Contrary to how it sounds, this was a good start. We were both still there. We had a lot of work to do: addressing her fear, discovering who she was, and finding the space to work out her skills, needs and wants. Her inability to have a positive relationship with herself and others compromised her ability to work and her leadership capability. The work we did together ultimately allowed her to connect with herself and others. It gave her the grounding and pathway to try again for that sought-after promotion.

In order to know ourselves, we need to receive feedback from others. Without it, the view we have of ourselves may be inaccurate. It's a bit like the blind spot we have in our cars. We reduce that blind spot when we receive feedback. Good feedback is a gift, because it gives us a true picture of our skills, faults, and talents.

The impostor phenomenon

Have you ever felt like you don't belong? As if your friends or colleagues are going to discover you're a fraud, and you don't actually deserve your job and accomplishments? Each year I used to remark to my accountant how lucky I was because I genuinely believed I had built my business out of luck. I completely ignored that my long list of clients was due to my own skill set and capability. It's sometimes called the impostor phenomenon, first identified in 1978 by psychologists Clance and Imes. It's the idea that you've only succeeded owing to luck, and not because of your talent or qualifications. Astoundingly, according to the *International Journal of Behavioral Science* (Sakulku, 2011), an estimated 70% of people experience impostor feelings at some point in their lives. No profession, gender or age is immune.

The fact that everyone else sees a highly capable individual where you see an inadequate fraud is a pretty good indicator that your inner dialogue bears little resemblance to reality. It doesn't matter how intelligent, talented or skilled you are right now, I have news for you: you are never going to consistently reach that insanely high bar you've set for yourself. Ever. To beat the impostor phenomenon you must adjust your self-limiting beliefs. In this context, self-limiting beliefs are the negative thoughts and feelings you have about yourself that are holding you back from reaching your potential. Everyone has unconscious rules in their head about what it means to be competent. These rules tend to begin with 'should', 'always' or 'never'. Rewriting your inner rule book with more reasonable requests of yourself is hands down the best place to start. Here are a few we all need to re-write:

- I should know everything in my field.
- I should get it right the first time.
- I should excel in everything I do.
- I should always know the answer.
- I should always feel confident.
- I should never make a mistake.
- I should never need help.

> **✎ Relationships in Action**
> Take some time out and note down in your Learning Journal:
> 1. What is in your Impostor Rule Book? Statements that start with should, always and never?
> 2. Work back through these. How can you rewrite these internal statements to be more helpful?

Dr Valerie Young, an internationally recognised expert on impostor syndrome, has conducted decades of research studying fraudulent feelings among high achievers. She uncovered several 'competence types' that people who struggle with confidence attempt to follow. Being aware of these types allows us to identify where we fit and start to manage them. Impostors don't all experience failure-related shame the same way because they don't all define competence the same way. Here are Dr Young's five different competence types, each with its own unique focus and flaw:

1. The Perfectionist – primary focus is on 'how' something is done. This includes how the work is conducted and how it turns out. One mistake equals failure and shame.

2. The Expert (the knowledge version of the Perfectionist) – primary concern is on 'what' and 'how much' you know or can do. Because you expect to know everything, even a minor lack of knowledge denotes failure and shame.
3. The Soloist – cares mostly about 'who' completes the task. It has to be you and you alone. Needing help is a sign of failure that evokes shame.
4. The Natural Genius – cares about 'how' and 'when' accomplishments happen. It's all about ease and speed. Not being able to bang out your masterpiece on the first try equals failure and, you guessed it, evokes shame.
5. The Superhuman – focus is on 'how many' roles you can juggle and excel in. You should be able to handle it all, perfectly and easily. Falling short in any role (parent, partner, friend, volunteer) evokes shame.

> ### ✎ Relationships in Action
> Take some time out and note in your Learning Journal:
> - Which competence type do you see yourself falling into?
> - Describe an alternative mindset that will better serve you.

Impostor syndrome relies on a head full of negative thoughts. I talked a little about negativity bias in the Self-Awareness Anchor. It is such an important point because our negative self-talk can stop us from reaching our full potential. One strategy to help with the thoughts in your head is to do the following:

1. Acknowledge your inner critic voice and what it is saying. Notice your thoughts and feelings – without judgement. Name them: 'I am noticing that I am feeling... worried/nervous/uncomfortable, etc.'

2. Examine your thoughts. Is it useful or helpful? It might be an old story. What does listening to this story do for you? Does it help you take effective action? Is it at odds with who you need/want to be?
3. Practise holding your thoughts 'lightly' (as if they are sitting lightly in the palm of your hand). Holding them tightly can make them feel like facts. Try saying, 'I notice that I am having a thought that …'
4. Respond to your inner critic saying, 'Thank you for your opinion, but I will act in line with my values.' Remember that your values underpin who you want to be, the things you want to do and what you want to stand for in life.

Trust in yourself

One small word that means so much! When we think about trust we usually default to thinking about trusting others, but first we need to learn to trust ourselves. I was fascinated to discover that the word 'trust' derives from a North Germanic language (used between the 8th and 11th centuries, back in the time of the Vikings) meaning 'confidence.' To distrust is to have no confidence in someone or something. Trust is at the core of every relationship. Trusting in ourselves and trusting in others are quite different to each other.

Trust in ourselves means we can back our decisions, no matter how tough they are. It also means living in line with our values and managing our urges. Psychotherapist Cynthia Wall says that when you trust yourself you are able to consistently take care of your own needs and watch out for your safety (2004). When people say, 'I just don't trust myself', they are saying that they don't have confidence to follow through on a commitment. I hide my stash of chocolate in the vain hope that I might forget it's there. I protect myself from myself. The reality is that I lack faith in my ability to not gobble down the whole block.

I know my judgement is solid. There have been times when I have made excruciatingly difficult decisions around my daughter's health and care. Without any guidance or playbook I have had to back my judgement knowing that the consequences were incredibly serious. At other times I've had to weigh up whether to trust my daughter to be safely on her own. Each time has been different and each time I had to make a decision and trust myself. There were times when my daughter didn't trust in herself and, fortunately, she was able to tell us. She trusted herself to seek help and implicitly trusted me to find it for her.

Why don't we trust ourselves? Part of the reason carries over from our childhood, when we really weren't that trustworthy. As adults, many of us continue to hold on to that script. As children, adults made us do the right thing, and not what we wanted to do. We were being trained to eventually do the 'right thing' on our own. Now we are in charge and can buy as much chocolate as we want, our inner child still wants to gobble it all up. The solution lies in giving ourselves the things we always wanted, openly and without retribution at the right time and place. When I want to eat chocolate, I need to engage my self-awareness to try and understand why I want to eat it. Is it to self-soothe? Is it because I just got back from a ten-kilometre run or is it because I am tired? When we pause from eating (or doing any action) blindly we give ourselves the space to acknowledge that we are doing it and ask, 'Should I be?' If the answer is yes, then we need to allow ourselves to enjoy it.

Values are at the heart of keeping commitments. When we commit outside of our values it is much harder to deliver. At the minute, I am trying to be a fit, healthy, well-rested mum who's trying to do a half-marathon in three months' time … but it's 11 pm and time for bed, not chocolate! When our decisions are out of alignment with our values it's hard keeping our word, which leads to disappointment in ourselves and lack of trust from others (see Values and Character Strengths in the Self-Awareness Anchor).

> ### ✎ Relationships in Action
> Take some time out now to answer these questions in your Learning Journal:
> - In which situations do you find it hardest to trust yourself?
> - What do you find the hardest to be honest with yourself about? You could ask those around you to help you with this question.
> - When do you struggle with your confidence?
> - What are you willing to do to help yourself be more trustworthy and confident in the above?
> - Take some time out to reflect on what that means for you.

All relationships take time, effort and good honest communication. Listen to how you talk to yourself. Notice how much of what you say is encouraging, and how much is critical. It's a good idea, and much easier, to start listening to yourself when things are going well. It gives you a great baseline and the opportunity to assess yourself objectively. Here is your starting point:

Discovery
- Be curious about yourself. There is a lot more going on behind the scenes than you may have thought about before.
- Start listening to yourself. Notice when you give yourself credit. Notice how you talk to yourself when things go badly.
- Respect yourself. Think of someone you respect and how you treat them. Turn it around and treat yourself that way.
- Actively listen to your body. How is it feeling? Notice the physical signs of your emotions.

- Notice your habits. Where do they come from? Do they still serve you?
- Improve your understanding of when you are motivated and when you are not.

Mindset
- Be prepared to go deep and really explore who you are.
- Be willing to compromise.
- Try not to judge yourself. You're here to observe and manage.
- Don't give up when things are hard. Remember that problems are problems because they are difficult.
- Engage in positive problem-solving and try new things playfully. If they work, great. If not, try something else.
- Learn from your mistakes – they are opportunities for improvement. Setbacks are normal.
- Be proud of the things you are doing well. Don't minimise their importance.
- It's okay to look after yourself. Choose some simple pleasures that you can include in each day.
- Find ways to say 'no' in line with your Purpose and values.
- Give yourself time. Time to learn these new skills. Time to grow.

✎ Relationships in Action

In your Learning Journal:
- List ten things that you love about yourself.
- Draw a box around them.
- Go back and refer to them often. Especially when you are feeling bad.

Workplace relationships

Work is a huge part of our lives. When work is not going well, life is not going well. It is easy to overestimate the importance of the 'what' we do, when 'who' we do it with is even more important. Even the most tedious jobs can feel fulfilling with nourishing relationships that provide a sense of purpose. You would think effective organisations are all about doing a collective task, right? What's so interesting is that social connections and belonging have been found to play a central role in fostering a sense of purpose and wellbeing in the workplace, as well as a major impact on performance and retention (Huppert, 2017). It is also why organisations now realise why they need to invest in developing their people. Good workplace relationships help you to get up and go to work each day. When we belong and feel valued, we experience less conflict and are better equipped to navigate well through challenges. It also boosts our self-esteem.

Healthy relationships need robust and honest conversations, where we feel supported, heard and acknowledged. Poor workplace relationships lead to mistrust, depression, loss of self-esteem and confidence, all of which can affect our performance. They can be the deciding factor to leave a job altogether, particularly if that poor relationship is with your boss. A Gallup poll of more than one million employed US workers found that the number-one reason people quit their jobs was because of a bad boss or immediate supervisor.

Workplace relationships rely on mutual respect, honesty, openness and trust. They need candid communication, an authentic openness to diversity, inclusion and new ideas. To bring all of this to a relationship you need emotional intelligence. You might remember reading about emotional intelligence in the Self-Awareness Anchor. It's about your ability to recognise your own feelings and those of the people around you. Once again, we're talking about looking both inward and outward.

A healthy team gets work done while their relationships remain intact. Team members are able to hold each other to account, address issues and manage poor performance. When conflict does arise, it is solution-focused, win-win and productive. The whole is greater than the individual parts and more can be accomplished. Yet workplace relationships are often a source of conflict. The focus can be on others rather than taking personal ownership. This too is a balancing act – knowing when to focus on external factors and when to look inside. The world we experience is a reflection of our values and beliefs. The way people react and treat us is generally a direct reflection of the way we behave and treat others. And just like that, we are back to the Self-Awareness Anchor.

Workplace conflict and difficult conversations

Conflict is any situation where people have incompatible behaviours, priorities, facts, methods, values, goals, interests, principles, feelings, etc. Managing conflict well is a skill we learn, it doesn't come automatically. We need to become conflict competent. In my coaching sessions I often hear people say, 'I avoid conflict' and 'I don't handle conflict'. The very first thing I ask people to do is look at what they're afraid of, and how it would be if they weren't. Without fear and well equipped with skill, what would they say and do differently? *Becoming a Conflict Competent Leader* by Craig Runde and Tim Flanagan is a really useful guide (it is expensive, so you may want to ask your library to order it in).

Poor past experiences might be a reason you avoid conflict. Intimidation and emotional or physical aggression hang around in your memory. Or you might think that being assertive will lead to aggressive behaviours. Perhaps you haven't thought much beyond the negatives to see that, when handled constructively, there are genuine opportunities in conflict. Conflict competence can resolve different opinions and lead to innovation.

There are two categories for responding constructively to conflict: actively and passively. Active responses can be used to directly engage the other person to resolve an issue. These help you reach out to them, understand their position, and generate solutions to the problem together. Here are some things you can try:

- Perspective Taking – put yourself in the other person's position, try to understand their point of view.
- Create Solutions – brainstorm with the other person, ask questions and try to create solutions to the problem together.
- Express Emotions – talk honestly with the other person, express your thoughts and feelings.
- Reach Out to the other person – make the first move, and try to make amends.

Passive responses, on the other hand can be useful while preparing to resolve a conflict. They can help you think things through before and during the conflict conversation, helping you both form a more receptive, calm and adaptive mindset. Here you can use:

- Reflective Thinking – analyse the situation, weigh the pros and cons, think about the best response.
- Delay Responding – wait things out, let matters settle down, or take a 'time out' when emotions run high.
- Adapt – stay flexible and try to make the best of the situation.

✏ Relationships in Action

To prepare for a challenging conversation, take some time out to answer the following questions in your Learning Journal:
- What kinds of things has this person said to you?
- Describe behaviourally how they express themselves (verbally and non-verbally).
- What is important to them? How do you know that?
- Why might they be responding this way?
- What have you tried so far? What was their response?
- What are their skills and abilities that you admire?
- What do they do that you don't admire?

Usually, an event kicks off the need for a difficult conversation. And often we dwell on it until we can't tolerate our feelings anymore before we address it. Sooner is better. The mindset for starting a difficult conversation is not about waiting for the courage, skill or confidence. It is about expecting to have these conversations with the discomfort. Feeling uncomfortable signals that this is an important conversation to you. It is also common to overestimate how hard the conversation will be. It's a bit like getting an injection. The worry beforehand is often a lot worse than the actual event. And the outcome is usually worthwhile.

Timing is key

I wish there were a formula for deciding when to have a difficult conversation. What I do know is that it is good to start before matters turn to the extreme. These conversations are all about feelings and we need to be clear on our Hot Buttons before we start (remember these from the Self-awareness Anchor). It also holds true that we need to have these conversations despite how we are feeling. Our feelings do not drive our behaviour. Many of us try our hardest to hide our feelings during these conversations. This just isn't possible in a difficult conversation; they come along with us no matter how hard we try to hide them. Our feelings leak. According to Block, only 7% of our communication is through words, 38% is through voice, tone, rate and inflection, and 55% is through face and body. So, it is important to give yourself an opportunity to express your feelings and find a way that you will be heard directly and clearly. Naming them is a great strategy: *I am feeling very angry and disappointed about this.*

Here are some things to prepare and include in your conversation:

- Find a relaxed place without interruptions.
- Don't wait too long before you have the conversation.
- Stick to the facts (not their intentions).
- Use specific examples of work or behaviour.
- Give your reasons for raising the issue.

- Remember to invite their side of the story.
- Brainstorm what you both can do differently in the future.
- Agree on one immediate action.

Trust at work

Trust in others is a tight bond. Over time it's a balancing act and can easily topple one way or the other. When there is mutual listening, consideration and care along with mutual respect and dependability, the balance of trust can withstand the odd wobble. Building trust is about keeping your commitment to the other person, so they feel safe and supported, doing what you say you will do. Trust creates an environment where conflict can be resolved constructively without damage to the relationship. Trust is when both actions and words align.

We know that trust is essential at work, but how do we know when we have it and how do we build it when it doesn't exist? Dr Paul Zak is a neuroscientist who has research linking the neurotransmitter oxytocin to the building of trust at work (2017). He examined brain activity as it was occurring in the most productive work teams and discovered that trust was a key factor. He describes trust as a kind of lubricant. When trust is high a little friction can be tolerated, but when trust is low a small amount of friction leads to poor performance, poor teamwork and disengagement. According to Dr Zak, when our brains release the neurotransmitter oxytocin, it signals to the brain that someone is trustworthy. This motivates us to reciprocate the trust and increases our sense of empathy, which is everything we need to be a good team member. Interestingly, testosterone, which is present with obvious and hidden aggression, bullying, exclusion and displays of dominance, inhibits the production of oxytocin. So does chronic stress. So, if you're under enough stress and your brain is in survival mode, you're not going to be a great team player, empathic or all that social.

David Maister, author of *The Trusted Advisor*, describes four components to trustworthiness, how much you are trusted (Maister et al., 2001). He presents a telling equation:

$$T = \frac{C + R + I}{S}$$

Credibility (and ability): credible ability, the demonstrable competence at doing your job. Usually the easiest to achieve. I can trust what you say, I believe you …

Reliability: consistent and predictable behaviour over many interactions to build familiarity of behaviour; your actions connect with your words. Acting with a set of principles that encompass fairness and honesty. I can trust you to …

Intimacy: how secure and safe you make people feel when they are sharing with you; the basis of a caring and trusting relationship. It is felt with emotions and is crucial to creating a safe space for vulnerability. Intimacy is more about who we are than any other aspect of trust. I feel comfortable discussing this issue with you …

Self-orientation: taps into your motives and self-interest. People need to know you've got their back, that you care. Excessive self-interest could show as finishing people's sentences or re-orienting the story to their circumstances.

Being credible, reliable and intimate builds trust. Self-interest destroys it. When we lose trust in someone, it tends to be because one or more of these requirements are seen to be lacking.

Networking

If networking makes you groan, stick with me, I will explain how and why it works. Hot tip: it doesn't require the type of intimate relationship-building which might be scaring you away. In fact, the opposite is true: networking relies on weak social ties. Think about your social world as having an inner circle and an outer circle. People in your inner circle are the people close to you, the ones you talk to often, while your outer circle is made up of acquaintances you see infrequently. Mark Granovetter, from Johns Hopkins University, named these categories strong ties and weak ties (1973). For new information and ideas, weak ties are more important than strong ones. In 1970, he surveyed people making job transitions and found that 83% of those who were successful in their search had managed it with the help of weak social ties.

When you connect exclusively to your strong social ties they are often connected like a cluster, to each other as well as to you. Weak social ties tend to be connected to other social clusters, which means they'll spread news of you to entirely different groups of people. As Granovetter pointed out, the people you spend a lot of time with swim in the same pool of information as you do. For professional success, you need to swim in a few other pools. We depend on friendly outsiders to bring us news of opportunities from beyond our immediate circles; the more we have, the better. Weak-tie interactions happen when we are out and about doing things. Let's reflect for a minute on Covid lockdown: it took away so many of those weak social ties that were helping us to feel happy.

> ### ✎ Relationships in Action
> Take some time out and note down in your Learning Journal:
> - your strong ties
> - your weak ties.
>
> Use your emails or contacts on your phone to help your recall these relationships.
> - What groups are/were you a member of?
> - Are there other interest groups you could join?

Building quality relationships

Humans are not born with the ability to develop and build great quality relationships with others. It is something we learn through trial and error, time and effort. And we keep learning, because perfect relationships don't exist. We can all learn to be better in our relationships by practising a few basic behaviours which, ultimately, build trust.

Listen well, without judgement or criticism. Park what you know to the side: you already know it. When you give someone the opportunity to share their thoughts you are helping them to feel heard and valued. Don't try to finish someone's sentences. Ask open questions that will deepen your understanding of what they are saying. It will encourage them to keep talking and talk to you next time. We naturally bond with people who take the time out to listen to us and want to spend time with us. We are put off by people who are too busy, distracted or self-interested.

Read a person's non-verbal cues to check that what they are saying aligns with the signals you are receiving. If someone says that they're okay, but it doesn't appear that way, you may wish to do an extra check-in with them. This tells them that you are paying attention to the whole person.

Pay attention to small details. People love it when you remember their name, especially when you've only met someone once or twice. They also feel valued when you remember a small, or large, detail about them. If your memory isn't the best, perhaps note down information in a book or your phone. Keeping a record also helps you keep your facts accurate.

Try not to overshare or undershare. It's best to pace yourself with what you are prepared to disclose. Oversharing is uncomfortable and sends signals to the other person that you are more interested in yourself than them. On the other hand, not sharing anything about yourself can also make people less willing to share their own stories. Healthy relationships include a mutual sharing of feelings.

Keep things positive. Act in line with your values. Gossip can be misleading and destructive. Start constructive conversations that help the other person feel empowered and good about who they are. They need to feel supported and cared for, especially if they are going through a bad time. After all, one day, you may need to be the recipient of someone else's care.

Anchor Self – Relationships

Take some time out to conduct your Relationships DIY Assessment.

Give yourself a score out of 10, where 10 is true all of the time and 1 is never true.

Relationships	1–10
I like who I am	
I support and encourage myself	
My self-talk is positive and encouraging	
I have trusted work relationships	
I have a solid group of friends to whom I am close	
There are a few work colleagues with whom I can truly be myself	
When I am going through difficulty, I always have one or two people who know	
I can have difficult conversations without negative repercussions	
Relationships TOTAL	

When you have added up your score, out of a total of 80, colour in your Relationships Anchor score on the circumplex. Use the Scoring Key as your guide. As you progress through this book, you can return to your assessment and continue to colour in the various Anchors.*

---

* At the end of the book, your individual Anchor scores can be translated across to form your Anchor Self-profile.

RELATIONSHIPS

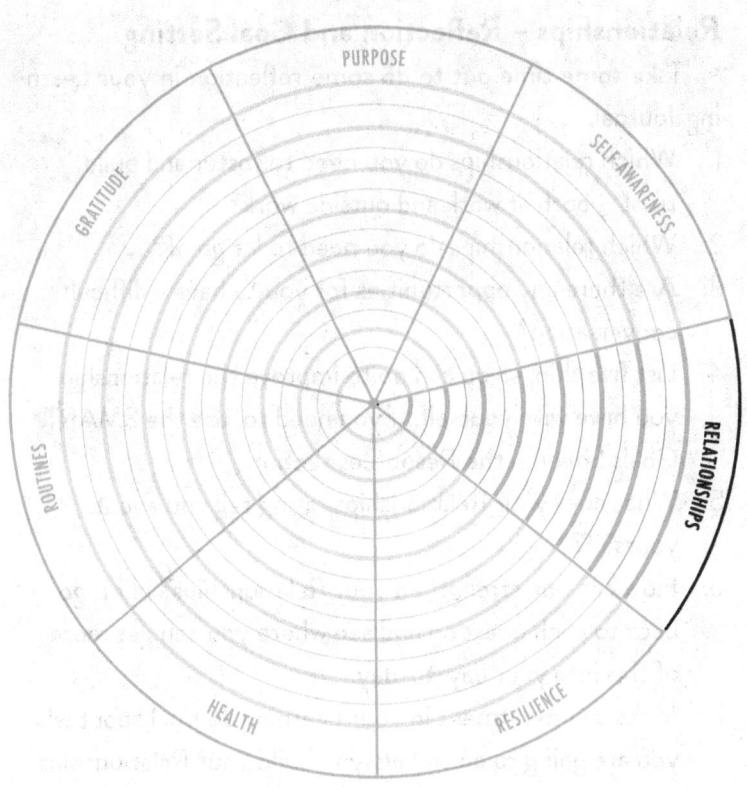

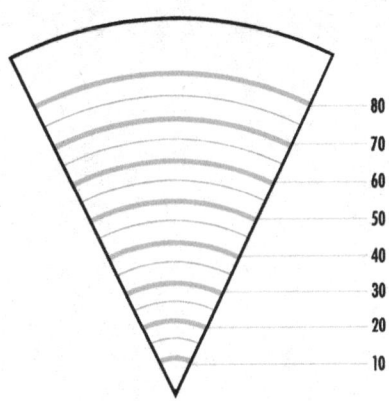

Scoring Key

Relationships – Reflection and Goal Setting

✎ Take some time out to do some reflection in your Learning Journal.

1. Which relationships do you need to foster and build trust – both at work and outside work?
2. Which relationships do you need to let go of?
3. Are there any opportunities for you to have a difficult conversation?
4. List five things you can do to improve the relationship you have with yourself. If you need to, use the SMART Goals Sheet in the Resources section.
5. What does your Relationships rating tell you about yourself?
6. How can you strengthen your Relationships? Hint: go back to each question and see where you can get more of this into your day-to-day.
7. Make a commitment in your Learning Journal about what you are going to do to help you build your Relationships Anchor.

8

Gratitude

*Gratitude is not only the greatest one but also
the mother of all the other remaining virtues.*
—Marcus Cicero (106–43 BCE)

In this chapter I share with you what the Gratitude Anchor is and why it's important. I'll take you through some of the research and some of the biggest obstacles to cultivating a gratitude attitude in your life.

Why is Gratitude important?

We might think of gratitude as a luxury, but it is actually necessary to living a great life. Do you want to just 'get through' life or do you want to experience joy, happiness and live a life 'on purpose'? Much of our time and energy is spent pursuing things we currently don't have. Gratitude reverses our priorities and helps us appreciate the people and things we do have.

Thank you, IKEA

I remember visiting IKEA with my daughter one Saturday to buy some picture frames. Nothing too big, mind you, because the boot of my car was already close to full. Not with ballet clothes or basketball gear or tennis racquets or any of the things an active 12-year-old girl would need for a regular sports-filled weekend. My boot was consumed by a great big black wheelchair. Normal weekend activities were out of our reach. It was not what thought I would ever have in my boot, and it certainly didn't fit my imagined weekends of a mother of a pre-teen daughter.

Instead, I learned the skill of conscientiously hunting for disabled parks. Next, I'd ensure the car was parked smack on the gutter so my daughter was close enough to lift herself into the wheelchair. She was heavy for me to lift and I wanted her to do as much for herself as possible. Life became about little adjustments. Parking my car, with my daughter in it, meant ensuring there wasn't a tree, a rubbish bin, another car too close, or a kerb too high, so that we could open the car door enough to navigate the big wheelchair into place. I was constantly running the risk of nails or glass becoming embedded in my tyres and found myself with a flat tyre every couple of months.

On this particular day, though, I was in a slump, feeling sorry for myself and for my daughter. With parking sorted, I lifted out the heavy, clunky wheelchair and realised, while assembling it (something else I now had down pat and did very quickly), that I had to pull myself together too. We chatted aimlessly as we made our way over to the lifts at the base of the store. When the lift arrived and its giant doors opened, we saw two of the largest wheelchairs I had ever seen. Each one had a disabled young adult strapped in place. One had breathing apparatus attached to his face, with bottles, tubes and bags hanging from the back of his chair. The young caregivers pushing the wheelchairs were laughing and chatting. This was the reality check I needed. Our situation was a long way from what I had just seen.

My attitude had needed a seismic shift. I'd been resentful when I needed to be grateful. It became clear to me in that moment that things can always be so much more difficult. I'd been consumed by what we didn't have, not with what we did. After all, we can have conversations and laugh together. She can tell me what she wants and fears. She can bathe and feed herself. Even though the only way she would get around the house was by crawling on her hands and knees, she could do so independently. In that moment, my thoughts about the wheelchair changed. It had given us the freedom to get out and about. I became grateful for all the things we did have. I started to actively look for all the things we could be grateful for. While I was doing so, I noticed how much better I was feeling. Feeling grateful changed my mood!

That visit to IKEA was a pivotal point for me. I realised how easy it is to focus on what we didn't have. This unhelpful thinking gave oxygen to negative thoughts and further amplified my bleak feelings which, in turn, obstructed both solutions and gratitude. By being grateful for what we did have, I gained so much. I knew the research on gratitude. I'd been teaching it in my workshops and even got my clients to keep gratitude journals, but I hadn't realised its power until that day. Since then, I've done my level best to keep my own daily gratitude journal.

What it is to be Grateful

Most people have an instinctive understanding of what gratitude is, but it can be surprisingly difficult to define. Is it an emotion, a virtue, or just a behaviour? It can mean different things to different people in different contexts. I am sure you have heard the term to 'be grateful' or 'have gratitude'. The word gratitude comes from the Latin 'gratia', which means grace, graciousness or gratefulness (depending on the context). It strikes me that gratitude encompasses all of these meanings: it is a thankful appreciation for what we receive, whether tangible or intangible.

Gratitude is popularised as being an essential part of living a good life. Yet I meet so many people who don't have a deep sense of what being grateful means or feels like. Gratitude replaces thoughts of what you believe you lack or desire. It helps you to focus, appreciate, emphasise and acknowledge what you already have and the goodness in your life. When we experience gratitude, we often recognise that the source of this goodness lies partially outside ourselves. As a result, gratitude helps us to connect with something larger than ourselves, whether this is other people, nature, or even a higher power.

People feel and express gratitude in multiple ways. They can apply it to the past by retrieving positive memories and being thankful for elements of childhood or past blessings. Or the present, by not taking good fortune for granted. And it can be applied to the future by maintaining a hopeful and optimistic attitude. The most exciting thing about gratitude is that you have it within you to successfully develop and cultivate it further. Plus, it grows stronger with use and practice.

What the research says

Over the past two decades scientists have made great strides toward understanding the biological roots of gratitude, the various benefits that accompany gratitude, and the ways that people can cultivate feelings of gratitude in their day-to-day lives. A growing body of research reveals that gratitude has the power to benefit your social-emotional health, subjective wellbeing, and lead to responsible decision-making, social awareness, relationships and longevity. The benefits of gratitude include improved sleep quality, pain reduction and immune system improvements, along with psychological conditions including depression and regulation of stress and anxiety.

As individuals, gratitude affects how we perform in the workplace, with higher job satisfaction, engagement, enhanced critical thinking, fewer sick days and demonstration of a more positive outlook. It increases our ability to problem-solve and be empathetic. It promotes engagement, positively impacts our relationships and assists in developing a healthy culture. The research builds a compelling case for the benefits of gratitude and why each and every one of us should go to great efforts to cultivate it, both in and out of work.

Gratitude is not simply the latest wellbeing buzzword (Tudge et al., 2016) – it has deep roots embedded in our evolutionary history (Bonnie & de Waal, 2004), our brains and DNA (Liu et al., 2017), and childhood development (Gleason & Weintraub, 1976). Neuroscience studies have identified areas of the brain involved in expressing and experiencing gratitude, providing a compelling case that gratitude is a core component of human experience (Zahn et al., 2014). Early studies have identified specific genes that may sit beneath our ability to experience gratitude (Algoe & Way, 2014). Other researchers have studied how gratitude develops throughout childhood. From a developmental perspective, even fairly young children have some concept of gratitude that develops as they mature. One US study found that children over 11 years spontaneously said 'thank you' while trick-or-treating four times more often than children younger than six years old (Gleason & Weintraub, 1976), suggesting that gratitude develops with age.

Research has linked personality and cognitive factors, and gender, to having a grateful disposition. Several studies have found that girls and women report feeling more grateful than boys and men, possibly because boys and men may be more likely to associate gratitude with weakness or indebtedness (Reckart et al., 2017; Froh et al., 2011). Other studies have identified certain traits that act as barriers to gratitude. These include envy, materialism, narcissism and cynicism (McCullough et al., 2002). One study looked at the negative relationship between materialism and life satisfaction, and found that the lower life satisfaction among materialistic people could be explained by the fact that they reported lower levels of gratitude (Tsang et al., 2014).

An innovative study that asked participants about their emotional state immediately after completing various gratitude exercises found that people felt both uplifted and indebted (Layous et al., 2017). There are now many studies suggesting that more grateful people are healthier (Jans-Beken et al., 2020), and that scientifically designed practices to increase gratitude can encourage healthier habits. Gratitude practices, like keeping a gratitude journal or writing a letter of gratitude, can increase happiness and overall positive mood. It inspires people to be more generous, kind and helpful (or prosocial) (Layous et al., 2017), which strengthens relationships, even romantic relationships. Research by Dr Robert Emmons found that regularly writing brief reflections on moments for which we're thankful can significantly increase wellbeing and life satisfaction. Regular grateful thinking can increase happiness by as much as 25%, while keeping a gratitude journal for as little as three weeks results in better sleep and more energy.

When you express gratitude, your brain releases a surge of dopamine, a neurotransmitter that plays an important role in many vital functions, including pleasure, reward, motivation, attention and bodily movements (Zahn et al., 2014). This surge of dopamine gives you a natural high, creating good feelings that motivate you to repeat specific behaviours, including expressing even more gratitude. It is also associated with increased serotonin production (Korb, 2015) which stabilises our mood and helps us feel more relaxed.

The Gratitude Toolkit

Topics covered:
- gratitude's biggest obstacle
- being grateful when sh!t is going on
- cultivating gratitude
- gratitude at work.

Gratitude's biggest obstacle

Having a high opinion of oneself has been seen as a big obstacle to feeling and expressing gratitude. Ungrateful people tend to have a sense of excessive self-importance, arrogance, vanity, and a high need for admiration and approval. This perversion of reality undermines the ability to freely accept life's gifts. At the more pathological end of the scale are narcissists, people who are profoundly self-absorbed and lack the empathy needed for entering into deep, satisfying, mutually enhancing interpersonal relationships. The more ordinary cohort includes people who just feel entitled to succeed and exempt from having to follow the rules. Special treatment is their expectation. Entitlement is the enemy of gratitude. It sounds like this:

- life owes me something
- people owe me something
- I deserve this.

We all have our moments of preoccupation with self, and without self-awareness it can cause us to forget our benefits and our benefactors.

Robert Emmons suggests that gratitude is an attitude, not a feeling that can be easily willed. Even if you are not satisfied with your life as it is today, he believes that if you go through grateful motions, the emotion of gratitude should be triggered.

✎ Gratitude in Action

In your Learning Journal do a quick assessment of how entitled you think you are:
- Do you think you are more deserving than others?
- Do you believe that you always deserve the best because you're worth it?
- Do you deserve to be 'let off the hook' every now and then?
- Do you believe you should be the first to be rescued, if in a dangerous situation?
- Do you believe that great things should come your way?

If you answered yes to more than four or five of these questions, you're going to find it quite difficult to be grateful.

Don't be disheartened: you can change your attitude to gratitude. You can learn to become more grateful and reap its benefits.

Being grateful when sh!t is going on

As I write today my daughter is an inpatient at a children's hospital about 25 minutes' drive from home. Melbourne is in Stage Four Covid-19 lockdown prohibiting travel further than five kilometres from home and we are under an 8 pm curfew. The hospital is 15 kilometres away. Driving along the deserted highway to visit her, I risk being pulled over by the police and having to justify the legitimacy of my actions and the purpose of my trip. I feel very uncomfortable. The idea of potentially having to justify my (legitimate) actions makes me feel ill.

Managing my thoughts is crucial to managing my behaviour in such a stressful time. I need to hold the feeling of guilt and of 'doing the wrong thing' lightly. I am allowed as a caregiver to travel to see my daughter. If I focus on the negatives and spend too much time thinking about all that is wrong with the situation, I could easily fall apart (emotional thinking). But my daughter and my son both need me (rational self-thinking). Plus, it won't be helpful to me. I won't make good decisions, at a time when good decision-making is crucial. I need to be fully present for my kids, and while driving! To get through this I need to start looking for the good in this situation, to find things to be grateful for and change my mood, behaviour and responses away from my negative thoughts.

Here is what I came up with:

- I am grateful that I live in a country with a health-care system that can support our family, and more critically my daughter, at this time.
- I am grateful that my daughter is in exceptional care, she is safe and she is loved.
- I am grateful that I have the capacity to visit and for my car that will get me there.
- I am grateful that the Covid-19 restrictions still allow me to visit my daughter, when I know many others are unable to visit loved ones.
- I am grateful that my son is old enough and mature enough for me to leave him by himself for the 90-minute return trip while I visit the hospital.
- I am grateful that my son supports and understands why I need to leave him to go to the hospital.
- I am grateful that I am well enough to care for myself and my son.

- I am also grateful for the amazing support I have from my friends who I can ring at *any* time for support or advice, or to just listen to me and give me strength.
- I am grateful that my piano teacher will still give me lessons over Zoom!
- I am grateful that I can still find time to focus on writing this book! It allows me to fulfil my need to help people be better.
- I am grateful that I can still work (thanks to Zoom and having flexible clients willing to work online).

When I allow myself to stop and think of things I am grateful for, and start to savour them, I start to feel better. I feel a lift in my mind and in my mood. If I focus mindfully on how I physically experience gratitude, it's like a wash of pleasure that floods into me. That's because neurologically, I am being flooded with oxytocin. When I remind myself of my role as a mum it allows me to be rational rather than emotional. It also protects me from having a limbic response and moves me into a pre-frontal cortex response, which is the part of our brain that allows us to make rational decisions. In limbic mode we think only of survival, which is why it is dangerous to allow ourselves to think in the negative for too long. Being grateful then becomes a very useful strategy that helps us get through the tough times. It is something that you can use both at home and at work.

✎ Gratitude in Action

Before you begin, out of 10, note down how you're feeling. In your Learning Journal, list 10 or 12 things you are grateful for.

Notice how you feel about each of them.

Describe those feelings.

Now note again how you're feeling out of 10. Have you improved slightly?

Cultivating gratitude

We are not always mindful of all our pleasures. Some things happen to us without us being aware of them. We don't always pay attention to the sensations of pleasure as we're eating, often more likely to throw the food down and get indigestion. We can only experience pleasure or gratitude when we take the time to acknowledge it. Savouring involves not just awareness but also a conscious attention to the experience. Savouring is a great way to create, extend and immerse ourselves in a stream of positive thoughts and emotions, and to access gratitude for that experience.

Before you start to practise fostering more gratitude in your day, here are a few things to keep in mind:

- Remember to be authentic.
- Acknowledge the small wins as well as the big ones.
- Gratitude can be achieved by anyone, including you.
- It is critical for you to live a great life.
- Saying thank you goes a long way.
- Attitudes take longer to cultivate than feelings.

The single, best thing you can do to develop your gratitude attitude is to keep a daily Gratitude Journal. By writing down three new things at the end of the day you are grateful for, you will train your brain to search for the positive. You may even find that you start collecting 'gratitudes' throughout the day that you can write in your journal of an evening. Reliving an event and thinking back over the positive event or thought will flood your brain with dopamine and help you feel good.

Here's a gratitude starter list:

- your health, your mind, your body and what you can do
- your work, your colleagues, your boss, your team
- your physical abilities, whatever they are
- your children, partner, family, friends, pets, community

- where and how you live, the roof over your head, your comfortable bed, clothes, shoes, fresh running water, the shower you had
- your ability to be flexible, to change how you do things
- your ability to communicate, to listen, to be heard
- the meal you ate, the drink you drank
- that you are focusing on living well
- difficulties that you have navigated well
- your learnings.

And so on! Just make sure you have a journal or a notepad and a pen by your bed so that the last thing you do before you turn the light out is write out those three new things you are grateful each day.

✎ Gratitude in Action

Take some time out to do The Five Senses Meditation.

Sit in a quiet place where you will be undisturbed and comfortable. Take a few deep breaths! Breathe in and hold for a few seconds, then release. Continue to expel all that used air. Do it again. Notice the feelings in your body as you begin to relax.

Close your eyes and think about what you love to taste, smell, see, feel and hear. What makes you feel happy when you notice these things crossing your path?

Allow a few minutes to let your mind wander over each sense. Think about three things you love in each sense:

- what your eyes can see
- what your ears can hear
- what your hands can touch and hold
- what you can taste
- what you can smell.

You can continue to be mindful of these things throughout your day.

> Try to notice your world from a sensory place: feel your senses and be grateful for them.
>
> How could you make changes to treat your senses and make them happier a little every day? Put perfume on; go smell that flower that you walk past. Notice the colour of the sky and how beautiful it is. How about that lovely birdsong outside the window? Or the wag of your dog's tail. The warmth from your daughter's hug, the sound of your son's laughter. A delicious meal.
>
> Being grateful for each of these senses can bring so much happiness into your life.

Here are some other tried and tested ways to develop gratitude in your life:

Gratitude Meditation: meditating involves focusing on the present moment without judgement. You can access gratitude meditations on apps such as Insight Timer, Calm, Smiling Mind. They have specific meditations on gratitude and they're terrific.

Say thank you: simply sharing two little yet powerful words has big psychological benefits for ourselves and others. If you are the giver, it creates a positive emotional state supporting the release of brain chemicals that make you feel good. For the receiver, research shows that people who are appreciated, by hearing a simple thank you, demonstrate a 50% increase in their willingness to help others.

Make sure your thank you is meaningful: here are a few tips to ensure that your thank you is meaningful and hits the mark. Firstly, take the time out to notice what others are doing. Be sure to make it specific and something that was above the call of duty, rather than what's generally expected. This demonstrates that you are noticing what people are doing, you are 'seeing' them. When you take the time to notice, it's easier to describe the effort they put in. Finally, let them know what it meant for you personally. Oh, and by the way, if the person you're thanking looks a little emotional, it may just mean that your gratitude hit the mark.

Write a gratitude note: you can make yourself happier and foster positive relationships with another person by writing them a letter expressing your appreciation for the impact that person has on your life. You can either send it or, better yet, deliver it and read it in person. To remind yourself to write gratitude notes, block out some time in your diary (say, once a month) to send at least one gratitude letter. It's also a lovely thing to occasionally write one to yourself. When one of my kids has done something that I appreciate I like to write a thank you on a nice piece of paper and either deliver it to them with a little treat, or I sometimes I just leave the note for them to find on the kitchen bench or on their bed.

Imagine thanking someone: our brains are very powerful but don't have the capacity to distinguish between imagination and reality. If you don't have the time to write a thank you, it's also possible to just think about thanking someone. You will need to imagine, as vividly as possible, that you are going through the motions of thanking that person. Research now supports that even going through the motions of thanking someone has positive benefits to wellbeing.

The gratitude visit: one of the most well-researched and validated examples of the positive outcomes that gratitude can have for wellbeing. According to one of the founding fathers of positive psychology, Dr Martin Seligman, the gratitude visit combines both introspective reflection and the outward expression of gratitude that will increase your happiness and reduce levels of depression in as little as a month. Seligman (2011) claims that a gratitude visit will increase our sense of wellbeing and enhance our relationship with the gratitude recipient. It also helps us shift our thinking about past events from the negative to the positive, prompting an immediate sense of wellbeing.

A gratitude visit consists of writing *and* (if possible) delivering a letter to a person you appreciate whom you have never properly thanked. The first task involves taking the time out to reflect on who that might be, then writing them a letter of gratitude. You will need to emphasise how they positively impacted you, how it helped you and how you still recall what they did. The second task involves giving them the letter. This is best done by a visit, if possible, and reading them the letter that you've written. This might feel a bit awkward or even embarrassing, but the positive benefits to both of you will far outweigh the potential awkwardness. If you give them the letter afterwards as a gift, it lets them revisit the moment at a later stage. Just remember, that even if you can't, for whatever reason, give the letter to them, you will still reap benefits from simply completing the first part of this exercise (the thinking about who, and then writing about the positive impact).

Be respectful: treat others in the same way that you would like to be treated. This will serve you well in your day-to-day expressions of gratitude. While we can express gratitude through directly telling someone we are thankful, how we conduct ourselves and our actions provide another avenue to reinforce our gratitude.

Express kindness: next time you're heading out to get a coffee, see if anyone else in the office would like one. You will let them know you value them, and chances are they will return the favour giving you the chance to be on the receiving end of some gratitude.

Experiential consumption: spending money on experiences rather than things. Several studies have found that people felt and expressed more gratitude following a purchase of an experience, such as concert tickets or dinner at a restaurant, rather than material gifts likes clothes or jewellery (Walker et al., 2016).

Avoid complaining: when we complain we reinforce a negative state of mind, making it more difficult to feel and express gratitude. We have a natural tendency to focus on the negative due to our brain's evolutionary hard wiring to focus on negative events (read about negativity bias in the Self-Awareness Anchor). The aim therefore is to focus on something positive, rather than complain.

Final tip: make time in your diary for your gratitude practices. If you're committing to a daily meditation, put it in your diary. If you're going to do a gratitude visit, put it in your diary.

Mr Grateful

In my coaching work, the clients who practise gratitude seem to really enjoy life and what they do. They are usually well liked by their colleagues and are seen to add great value to their organisation. They are often top performers. One client who comes to mind is what I would deem to be a very successful senior executive. He is the Operational Lead for the division of a software company he founded. What makes him stand out is that he is driven to perform better in order to repay the organisation that bought his company. He epitomises gratitude. He is kind and considerate, while being an extremely savvy and strategic businessperson. He balances the care of his staff and their demanding workloads with the organisation, stakeholder and customer needs. He is a super guy and an absolute delight to coach.

This man views the world through a lens of gratitude, but it is not forced. He leads with it. The display of his gratitude is almost incidental, yet it contributes to his success. For example, when he's talking about his boss, who can be difficult to work for, he consistently searches for the good in him. This is not to say that he is unaware of his faults and foibles, far from it! He approaches his boss with total respect coupled with an attitude of 'how can I support him so that he too may be effective here?' If he does happen to say something negative about his boss, he will always add a caveat with several positives. My client has an empathetic viewpoint of his boss and is genuinely and overtly grateful for the work that his boss is trying to achieve, rather than what he's failing to achieve. Every time we have a session he tells me how grateful he is for our conversations that help him navigate his role more effectively.

I am aware that having this high level of gratitude may not come naturally, but the rewards are irrefutable. As with any new habit or thinking style, make a conscious choice to weave it into your daily practice of life.

Gratitude at work

The practice of gratitude, and its close sibling appreciation, has started to infiltrate workplaces, from Facebook to Campbells Soup Company.

According to the *Washington Post*, Facebook founder Mark Zuckerberg set himself a personal challenge to write a thank you letter every day to staff for a year (McGregor, 5 February 2014). Douglas Conant inherited a mess when he became CEO of Campbell's, but he managed to turn the failing business around by 'walking the floor' and interacting meaningfully with as many employees as possible. He wrote up to 20 notes a day to employees celebrating their successes and contributions. He wrote over 30,000 thank you letters to his 20,000 staff over his tenure. 'This practice showed people that I was paying attention, that I was "all in",' he said (Conant, 2011).

Despite the positive benefits of gratitude, people are less likely to show gratitude at work than anywhere else, according to a 2013 John Templeton Foundation survey of 2000 workers. They found that most people felt better when they were thanked, but their mood improved when they thanked another worker. Despite the obvious benefits, some 60% of workers never express gratitude to their colleagues. The survey found that 81% of respondents would work harder for a more grateful boss. While expressing thanks to colleagues might feel awkward or even at odds with some workplace cultures, many organisations have been developing innovative ways to overcome those barriers. Building a culture of gratitude can transform our work lives.

Gratitude in the workplace builds professional commitment, efficiency and productivity. According to Chowdhury (2021) employees who express gratitude at work are more likely to proactively seek additional tasks and go the extra mile to complete their work. Gratitude improves a leader's compassion, consideration, and empathy. It appears to help staff be more effective and feel greater satisfaction. It can cultivate patience, with ourselves and others. Through gratitude you will be in a better position to make long-term decisions and set more meaningful goals, both at work and at home.

It goes without saying how important it is to regularly show the people we work with that we are grateful for their work, but it needs to be timely and authentic. Don't wait and be specific. Keep it as close as possible to the event you are grateful for and show them that you noticed the detail. Perhaps most importantly, there needs to be some heart behind your words. Inauthentic gratitude will likely do more damage than good. It can take the form of everything from a simple, brief nod to someone who helps answer a puzzling challenge, to a broad acknowledgement of a team that has worked tirelessly on a lengthy problem. Make it a regular habit.

Here are a few ideas to build a culture of workplace gratitude:

- Start at the top: when staff know that their bosses appreciate them they work harder and get more done. Working from the top down is the best way to cultivate gratitude into your organisation. More than 90% of employees surveyed by the John Templeton Foundation said that they would view a grateful boss as a successful person.
- Resource your staff: ensure that your staff have all the necessary resources to be successful and effective in the workplace. Your staff will be grateful that you are giving them the tools for success and seeing value in their work.
- Gratitude sharing in meetings: start weekly meetings by asking each team member to share something at work they feel grateful for. This will help the team to connect with each other.
- Thank you note: sharing a thank you note or email positively reinforces the behaviour you wish to see and helps you feel good. It helps to build positive relationships with your colleagues and your team. Try to write a handwritten note for even greater impact.
- Remember those who rarely get thanked: there are people in every organisation who are often overlooked for what they do. Take the time to let people know (wherever you go) – the cleaners, the drivers, the accountants, support staff, admin,

repairmen, catering staff, contractors and so on – that you are grateful for their contribution, no matter how small.
- Daily opportunities: search out opportunities throughout your day for small acknowledgements of gratitude. There are plenty of them.
- Gratitude journal: the benefits of a workplace gratitude journal will help you to feel more satisfied and increase wellbeing. And it will boost your interactions with others.
- Mental gratitude: if you don't have time to write a thank you note you can mentally thank a team member whose work positively impacts you. Simply thinking about being grateful and imagining that you are saying thank you is almost as beneficial to you as actually doing it. Remember to go ahead and say thank when you do get a chance.

'I am happy because I'm grateful. I choose to be grateful. That gratitude allows me to be happy.'

—Will Arnett

Anchor Self – Gratitude

Take some time out to conduct your Gratitude DIY Assessment.

Give yourself a score out of 10, where 10 is true all of the time and 1 is never true.

Gratitude	1–10
I have a very long list of things to be grateful for	
When I'm going through difficulties, I always think of the good things that I have	
I am always grateful for the gifts and talents I have	
I always offer thanks and/or prayers for what I have received	
Being grateful helps me navigate through difficulties	
I am grateful for the opportunity to contribute to finding better solutions	
I highly value the friendship and love I get from people close to me	
I always acknowledge my appreciation to others at work	
Gratitude TOTAL	

When you have added up your score, out of a total of 80, colour in your Gratitude Anchor score on the circumplex. Use the Scoring Key as your guide. As you progress through this book, you can return to your assessment and continue to colour in the various Anchors.*

---

* At the end of the book, your individual Anchor scores can be translated across to form your Anchor Self-profile.

GRATITUDE

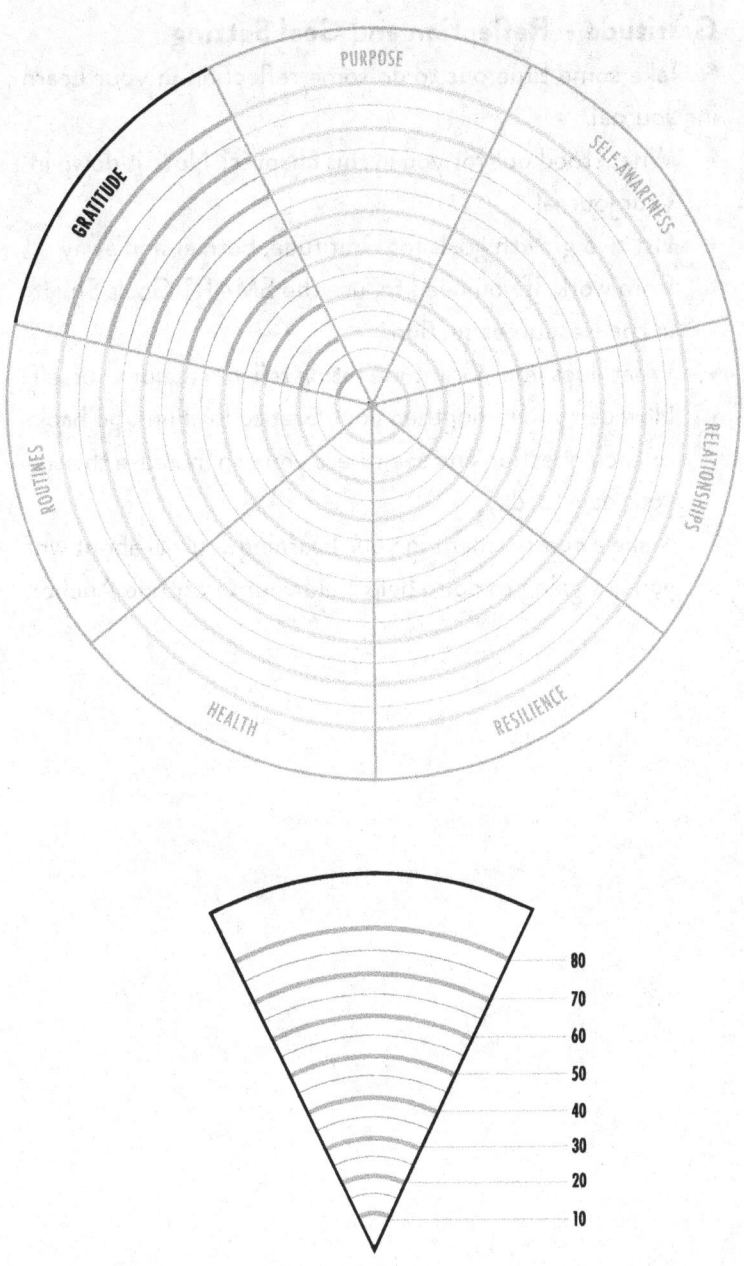

Scoring Key

Gratitude – Reflection and Goal Setting

✎ Take some time out to do some reflection in your Learning Journal.
- What stood out for you in this chapter? Note it down in your journal.
- List two growth goals for Gratitude, both at and away from work. If you need to, use the SMART Goals Sheet in the Resources section.
- What does your Gratitude rating tell you about yourself?
- How can you strengthen your Gratitude? Hint: go back to each question and see where you can increase this in your day-to-day.
- Make a commitment in your Learning Journal about what you are going to do to help build your Gratitude Anchor.

9

Health

Health is something that we often take for granted, simply because our brains can apply themselves to the task without our input. Taking care of our health is a vital anchor for maintaining a great life. This chapter covers some key areas to look after both our minds and our bodies. The 7 Anchor Model is designed to help you live well above base level. It's a guide to live well and have a great life across our physical and mental health.

Why is Health important?

Just because you're not sick, doesn't mean you are healthy. The World Health Organization defines health as: 'A state of complete physical, mental and social wellbeing and not merely the absence of disease or infirmity.' Mostly, we don't pay enough attention to managing or monitoring our basic daily needs: sleep, diet and exercise. Back in the early days when I was a counselling psychologist, I would say, 'Never let yourself get too tired, too hungry or too thirsty'. The saying holds true no matter what's going on in your life. Whether life's feeling tough or you're flying high we shouldn't let ourselves get too tired, too hungry or too thirsty. Maslow's Hierarchy of Needs states that the biological requirements for human survival are air, food, drink, shelter, clothing, warmth, sleep. All the other needs become secondary until these primary needs are met. Without them our bodies don't function optimally.

With optimum health, we have a state of complete and balanced emotional, physical and spiritual wellbeing. It is a vital anchor for living a great life. Fortunately, even though many of us take our physical body for granted, it still maintains and preserves us. In Bill Bryson's book *The Body* (2019) he reminds us that it '… works 24 hours a day without (for the most part) needing regular servicing or the installation of spare parts, runs on water and a few organic compounds … Yet in some kind and miraculous way our bodies look after us, extract nutrients from the miscellaneous food stuffs we push into our faces and somehow hold us together, generally at a pretty high level, for decades. Suicide by lifestyle takes ages.'

An (un)Healthy body

Watching my daughter's body deteriorate and wither, after being in a wheelchair for a dozen or so months, was incredibly confronting and challenging. It was a daily visual reminder that she was unwell. It also flew against how I had lived my values of looking after my body and those of my children. I come from a healthy, strong family, modelled by my own parents. Looking after ourselves was integrated into our lives. Running, moving and being active was part of what we all did every day. My father was a marathon runner. My mother, before she became unwell, was an avid tennis and golf player. Even with her illness she would push herself daily to go to the gym doing whatever she could right up until the months before her passing. My daughter's health condition came on suddenly just after her 12th birthday; she was barely able to get around the house. After six months and with withering muscle tone she needed a wheelchair. The sight of her shrinking calf muscles was hard to fathom, given the physio exercises she was doing.

Initially, I too let my fitness and diet deteriorate. Prior to my daughter's illness I would think nothing of going for a 15-kilometre run or a yoga class together with twice-daily dog walks. I lost the discipline I'd had my whole life and my body quickly began to develop its own problems. I would wake up with pins and needles in my arms and hands.

I developed body stiffness, aches and back pain. A nerve conduction test, however, assured me that there was nothing sinister going on. Suddenly my clothes didn't fit. I'd never experienced health issues or weight gain before. Friends and colleagues would say, 'It's not surprising that you're feeling like this, you're under so much stress and have been for so long!' But no-one really came to me with a solution.

The reality was that my daughter and I were missing out on the benefits from exercise – the body's natural painkillers, mood elevators and feelings of relaxation and optimism. We both needed them! I had to start looking after myself again, so that I could help stop her body deteriorating any further. I would need a healthy mind and a healthy body to manage this difficult situation for myself and both of my children. I re-introduced running, a quick way to help me feel better again. My fitness returned and the benefits flowed. The simple choice of moving again helped me live a much better life and be a better mum.

Helping my daughter was going to be a little trickier. I wanted her to have enough muscle tone when (if) she was going to walk again. We worked with what she could do. Daily hydrotherapy gave her the opportunity to exercise without having to bear her own (tiny) weight. It was tough for her. Physical touch caused her pain; even the pressure from the pool water on her skin hurt. When I asked if she enjoyed her swim, she'd just look over and say, 'Mum! There's nothing enjoyable about this!' But we were on the same page: she wanted to be ready to walk when she could. She was willing to push herself to be better despite how she was feeling. Her courage was extraordinary. And of that I am still very proud.

Impact of stress on Health

Stress comes in many forms and produces many symptoms, from mild through to life-altering. It can look like this: physical anguish, heart palpitations, tense muscles, fidgeting, taut facial expressions, headaches, jaw pain, neck pain and back pain, dry mouth, lump in your throat, pale, sweaty or clammy skin. Or perhaps intestinal symptoms: butterflies, heartburn, cramps or even diarrhoea. A pounding pulse, chest tightness and rapid breathing are all part of the stress club. It can cause hyperventilation leading to tingling in the face and fingers, muscle cramps, light-headedness and even fainting. It seems that stress can do whatever it wants with your body and it can feel so awful that it creates further mental stress.

Before you know it you are caught in a loop where the mind and body compound each other's distress signals, creating a vicious and unpleasant cycle of tension and anxiety. When stressors are always present, your body's reaction stays switched on. Long-term activation of your stress-response system can disrupt almost all of your body's processes, putting you at increased risk of:

- anxiety
- depression
- digestive problems
- headaches
- heart disease
- sleep problems
- weight gain/loss
- memory and concentration impairment.

The good news is that the body's stress-response system does resolve and your hormone levels return to normal once the stressor has passed. As adrenaline and cortisol levels drop, your heart rate and blood pressure return to baseline levels, along with other systems in your body. The more we understand about the emotional root cause of your stress, the more quickly we can reduce problems and modify behaviours that trigger stress.

What the research says

There is a mountain of research demonstrating the link between good physical health and good mind health, which are both key to living life well. All of the concepts I talk about in this chapter are so closely interrelated that the same results keep coming up in each area of research. Exercise is linked to physical and mental health, as are connection, rest, play, mindfulness and sleep.

Studies to date suggest that mindfulness improves our mood (Broderick, 2005), increases positive emotions (Geschwind et al., 2011) and shows promising effects in decreasing anxiety (Hofmann et al., 2010). It has been found to lower emotional exhaustion, burnout and increase job satisfaction (Hülsheger et al., 2013). Early studies suggest that mindfulness improves heart health (Levine et al., 2017) and may decrease cognitive decline from ageing or Alzheimer's (Quintana-Hernández et al., 2016). Meditation has also been found to increase attention in older adults (Malinowski et al., 2017). Mindful practice allows us to appreciate and connect more with the world around us, which in turn makes us less self-centred.

Our bodies and minds need exercise. According to the US Centers for Disease Control and Prevention regular exercise is an important part of leading a healthy life. It is one of the easiest ways to reduce our risk of chronic disease and improve the quality of our lives. It helps keep our brains healthy and improves memory across all age groups. Exercise lowers blood pressure, cholesterol, blood sugar, and improves heart health and sleep quality (Hower et al., 2018; Gordon et al., 2018). It improves joint pain and stiffness, helps maintain muscle strength and balance (two things that naturally deteriorate with age) and manages weight. It has been successfully used to treat anxiety disorders and clinical depression (Ströhle, 2009).

We can also learn a few things from kids about how our bodies and minds work together. There is a growing body of research on the value of play. Dr Peter Gray considers it to be an attitude that extends to all life situations and modifies how we perceive, evaluate, and approach situations. He notes that we might be more respectful of play if we regarded it as a self-motivated practice of life skills. Creativity, curiosity, being pleasure-filled, having a sense of humour, and spontaneity are all characteristics of play (Gray, 2015). It helps us to be open-minded, solve problems, confront difficulties in a novel way and accept failure. (Guitard et al., 2005). Without play, we start to imagine a stereotyped inflexible, humourless person who lives without irony and loses the capacity for optimism. This is a natural set-up to stress, violence or depression (Brown, 2009).

Life can't be all work and play: rest is important as well. According to Dr Alex Pang (2018), our productivity and creativity is impacted by what we do when we are not consciously working and thinking. Pang describes the importance of deliberate rest, where we are engaged in restful activities that recharge us. The phrase 'deliberate rest' comes from 'deliberate practice'. Anders Ericsson, an internationally recognised researcher in the psychological nature of expertise and human performance, famously coined the concept of deliberate practice. It is about the structured, regular, mindful practice that turns people into outstanding performers. Ericsson found that, on average, about 10,000 hours of deliberate practice was necessary to become a great violinist, inspiring Malcolm Gladwell's 10,000-hour rule. Gladwell observed that Bill Gates, the Beatles and lots of other creative people also get 'great' after 10,000 hours of programming or playing in nightclubs.

Even though the research has been around for a while, it took Covid to truly reveal the deep value of connection. Research has found that the social environment that shapes human health and social adversity, is closely linked to health and mortality (Snyder-Mackler et al., 2020). Strong social connections lower the rates of anxiety and depression, increase self-esteem, improve our empathy, and help build more trusting and quality relationships (Lane, 2001).

Health Toolkit
Topics covered:
- healthy minds
- exercise
- connection time
- play

- flow and focus
- deliberate rest
- sleep.

Healthy Minds

Information about eating for physical health can be found everywhere, but guidance for a healthy mind is slightly more elusive. Mind health is both difficult to assess and easy to overlook. To live and lead well, to optimise brain matter and create wellbeing, we need to take care of our minds and our bodies. Perhaps what most people don't realise is that activities for good physical health are helpful for good mind health. When we incorporate the following things *each day*, we can strengthen our brain's internal connections along with our external connections with other people:

- nutrition
- exercise
- connection time
- play time
- flow/focus/engagement time
- deliberate rest
- mindfulness
- downtime
- sleep.

✎ Health in Action

Take some time out to answer the following questions in your Learning Journal:
1. Think of five things you can do to look after your physical health.
2. Think of five things you can do to have a healthy mind.
   Of these ten things, put a star against those you do *on a daily basis*.

> Do you notice a difference between how you look after your physical health and your mind health?
> Reflect on why this may be.

It's all about finding a balance that works for you. Stressing about incorporating these things into each and every day becomes counter-productive. Simply do good things for yourself when possible. If one day you can't, then make the next day a fresh start and try again. By varying how and on what you focus your attention, you give your brain lots of opportunities to develop in different ways. Your brain is continually changing in response to focus and attention.

> ### ✎ Health in Action
> Ask yourself the following questions and write your answers in your Learning Journal:
> 1. Of the healthy mind activities, which ones do I do most days and which ones do I have trouble with?
> 2. Which activity am I willing to include in my daily practice to improve my mind?
>
> Set a 21-day SMART* goal around that.

Now it's time to talk mindfulness – a set of psychological skills for effective living that involves paying attention with openness, curiosity, kindness and flexibility (Harris, 2019). It involves accepting and paying attention to our current situation: what we can hear, touch, see and taste, including our thoughts, images and current feelings. Mindfulness can help us manage our response to emotions, and decrease stress,

---

* You can find more information on how to set a SMART goal in the Resources section at the back of this book.

anxiety and depression by dampening the activity in our amygdala. It slows our body down and quietens down the busy Default Mode Network in our brains. Mindful practice allows us to appreciate and connect more with the world around us, shifting us away from being self-centred. To be mindful helps achieve flow state.

At its most basic, mindfulness is doing one thing at a time and observing it with all of your senses. For example, finish the draft paper before checking your phone: clean your teeth and concentrate on that one activity. Don't do anything else. The practices of mindfulness are simple, but not always easy to incorporate into each day. Below are a few tips to start.

✎ Health in Action

1. Move your devices away from you to eliminate distractions.
2. Stop what you are doing.
3. Take a deep breath.
4. Notice how it feels.
5. Take another deep breath.
6. Notice how it feels. Does it feel different to the first? A tiny bit deeper maybe.

Create mindful activities throughout your day. Notice the sensations and see if you can allow yourself to fully get into the experience. Enjoy the experience! (Washing the dishes comes to mind.)

Choose an activity to pay attention to. It may be a simple stroll in your backyard or a walk down the hallway in bare feet. Practise holding your awareness on one thing and notice what comes up.

Nutrition

Having and maintaining a healthy diet offers significant rewards: from strong bones and teeth, to improved mood, memory, gut health and sleep. While most of us have a fairly good idea of what constitutes a healthy eating plan, not all of us have one. A healthy eating plan will fuel your body and help your mind to stay focused and effective throughout the day. The good news is that you have control over your diet. Across each and every micro-decision throughout the day, you have the power to choose healthy food.

Let me tell you about Jim. Every Friday, on his way home from the gym, Jim would stop at McDonald's for a Big Mac, large Coke, fries and hot-fudge sundae, as a reward. He told me that his weekly swim and Macca's session was a Friday night tradition. Clearly, going to the gym was a good habit. But we worked out that his 10-minute McDonald's treat was adding up to a whopping 1700 high-GI calories. Until our conversation, he hadn't even given it a thought. He also mentioned that he regularly looked for more food when he got home, as well as a few end-of-the-week bevvies. At the same time, he confided that he wasn't physically comfortable and knew he needed to carry less weight. Jim needed to replace his habit with something else. He decided to give up his weekly McDonald's visit and, instead, put that money into the charity jar he kept in his gym locker. He didn't break his habit, he replaced it. Ultimately, he benefited. The charity benefited. And so did his family, who started eating their Friday night meal together.

Breakfast is another important time for good habits. To kickstart your metabolism breakfast should be eaten before 8 am. As easy as it is, rushing out the door with a coffee doesn't do you any favours. Low-GI, high-protein foods are great kickstarters: oats or muesli, yoghurt, fruit, eggs or baked beans on toast. Highly processed sugary cereals just don't give you sustained energy. When you start the day with sugar you tend to crave sweet things for the rest of the day. The best strategy is to delay having any sort of processed sugar for as long as you can in your day. When you have a good breakfast, you should start to feel slightly peckish a few hours later. This is a sign your body is burning its fuel efficiently. It's also the time to have healthy snacks handy, like some yoghurt or a piece of fruit.

Mindfulness works hand in hand with nutrition. When we think consciously about the quality and amount of food we are eating, it becomes easier to make good food decisions. Where was the food sourced? What are its ingredients? How many ingredients and colours are in it? How fresh is it? Is this the portion size I really need? Setting ourselves up by creating good healthy habits and planning ahead helps us navigate through those really difficult times.

✎ Health in Action
Answer the following questions in your Learning Journal:
1. How often do you eat a meal you haven't prepared yourself: breakfast, lunch and dinner?
2. Of your takeaway meals, find out how many calories those meals contain (inclusive of your drinks – coffee, juice, etc.). You can probably find a recipe online for the home-made equivalent that shows the number of calories. Compare them.
3. How much do you spend on takeaway food each week? How much is that each month? What would be the annual figure?
4. What are you willing to do differently/adopt/give up, to eat more healthily?

I'm not suggesting that you become a calorie counter, but they do offer a handy metric to help you compare eating habits and learn how to manage your diet. A Big Mac has 508 calories, and if you add in the medium fries and a regular Coke, you're up to 1015 calories. A medium banana has 99 calories and it would take 28 minutes to walk off those calories if you are a 35-year old female who is 170 cm tall and weighs 65 kg. It goes without saying that the food quantity (portion size) and quality (fresh, locally sourced with minimal processing or additives) are the keys to a good diet. As a matter of interest, for a healthy, balanced diet, a woman needs around 8400 kJ (2000 cal) a day to maintain her weight. For a man, that figure is around 10,500 kJ (2500 cal) a day. You can see that these values vary depending on age, metabolism and levels of physical activity, among other things. So, generally speaking, breakfast needs to be around 400 calories, morning tea around 150 calories, lunch 450–500 calories, afternoon snack around 150 calories, and dinner between 550–650 calories. And if your current diet is working for you, great news. Keep up the good work!

Some tips for eating well:

- Plan out your snack and mealtimes – set an alarm if you have a habit of skipping meals and regretting it later. Not eating can affect your alertness and productivity.
- Divide food into 'everyday' foods or 'occasional/not at all' foods. Everyday food is balanced and nutritious, containing protein, fibre, healthy fats, fruits and veggies. Don't buy anything that your great-grandmother wouldn't recognise. Leave the highly processed foods for 'occasional' foods.
- If there is something you just can't resist, don't eliminate it completely. You don't need to feel guilty about eating something you love. Enjoy it, in moderation. Think about spending a month without it once a year and ask those around you to help you. Reward yourself at the end – in moderation.
- Avoid dehydration. Drink plenty of fresh water throughout the day. Nothing fancy, just good old clean water. The aim is for around two litres or eight glasses a day. You will need more if you exercise heavily. Water

will help avoid fatigue and headaches, keeping you productive.
- Reduce the sugar. Avoid fruit juices and fizzy drinks, as they fast-track your sugar consumption.
- Focus on portion size. Serve up the amount you intend to have. Some foods are designed chemically to make you want more. Don't eat from the packet.
- Try the healthy plate approach. Fill half a plate with non-starchy vegetables, one-quarter of the plate with a lean protein (poultry, seafood, beans, eggs, tofu, cottage cheese or Greek yoghurt) and one-quarter with a high fibre carbohydrate (fruit, whole grains or starchy vegetables).
- Be mindful of what you eat. Just eat and only eat. Not at your desk. Not driving. Not in meetings. Take a break from your work to relax and enjoy your meal.

Exercise

Sorry, I can't today. My brother's friend's grandmother's nephew's sister's aunty's pool cleaner's fish died. And yes, it was tragic.

Excuses are easy to find, but the truth is almost any type of exercise is beneficial. Exercise reduces the level of stress hormones, such as adrenaline and cortisol, in our bodies (Kraemer et al., 2020). It stimulates the production of endorphins that help us feel good and manage pain. You might have experienced the natural 'high' after a hard exercise session. It can both exhilarate and relax. Exercise boosts your energy, helping you achieve your goals, which leads to greater self-confidence. A simple 30-minute stroll can clear the mind and reduce stress. More active workouts can burn stress and calories.

It starts with your Why? You might be someone who struggles with exercise, but if you have a good reason, you're less likely to find an excuse. What is your personal need to exercise? Any goal is easier to maintain with internal drive, and almost impossible to maintain without it. Someone telling you to do it just isn't enough.

> ### ✎ Health in Action
>
> Take some time out in your Learning Journal to create your own personal rationale for being fit and healthy.
>
> Start by imagining that you are already fit and healthy. If you are, fantastic, you can use this exercise to maintain or tweak your routine.
>
> 1. List what you will be able to do as a result of being fit and healthy – be as extensive as you like here. Think across all the roles you play in your life.
> 2. Describe how that makes you feel.
> 3. Why is it important? Who benefits?
>
> Your reasons will likely align with the sort of person you want to be and need to be, and they will help you fulfil your purpose. For example, one of the reasons I like to be fit and healthy is to keep up with my kids.

Even in the middle of a pandemic, the Australian government listed exercise as one of the four reasons someone could leave their home during lockdown. Where I lived, the most locked-down city in the world, we were still allowed out to exercise for one hour each day. I know what you're thinking, but regardless of your circumstances there is always something you *can* do. You can remove obstacles, excuses and exercise blockers by facing them head on. There really is always something you can do. Here are the Heart Foundation's top six exercise excuses, along with some suggested solutions:

1. **Too tired**: your brain doesn't distinguish between mental and physical fatigue so it feels the same. Working at your desk all day may make you feel tired, but not physically. How could it?! While you think you need to slump on the lounge, just knowing that you are mentally rather than physically tired helps clarify what you need.

Exercise will boost your body battery. Committing to exercising with someone else might just motivate you to get out the door.

2. **I can't afford a gym**: Gyms can be expensive. Consumer website Finder revealed Australian's spent on average $21 per week (plus joining fees) on gym memberships in 2021 ($1100 per year). Of the 32% of Australians who have gym memberships, only 40% attended more than twice a week, and half went less than once a week. On the average yearly membership, this equates to $91 per visit. Anything is expensive if you don't use it. Look for alternative affordable forms of exercise, such as free and inexpensive online options through YouTube, Netflix and so on. Exercising does not need to cost money.

3. **No time**: It's easy for exercise to slip to the bottom of the list when we have such busy schedules. We all have the same 24 hours in a day, but what matters is how we choose to use them. Look for exercise opportunities in the in-between spaces in your day. Try walking to the shops rather than driving or 'walk and talk' when making calls. Go for an evening stroll after dinner. Mix your social time with exercise: instead of coffee with friends, make it a walk with friends.

4. **Waiting to be motivated**: Our brains like us to be comfortable, so they are not likely to shift us off the couch. Your commitment, rationale and goals are your motivation. Track your exercise progress to motivate yourself.

5. **Don't like exercising alone**: Neither do I. Finding a friend to exercise with a few times a week is a great way to stay accountable. Having a regular weekly commitment with friends across your week will provide extra incentive. You could join a fitness, running or hiking group, sign up to a team sport or join a yoga class. Only a few years ago I was

invited to play beach volleyball. I'd never played before and was quite nervous, but the team were lovely and taught me along the way.
6. **No fun/I get bored**: What do you find fun? Make a list of the exercises you like or have always wanted to try. There's plenty to choose from: hiking, yoga, swimming, basketball, dancing and gardening, just to name a few. If you're limited to a treadmill or an exercise bike, listen to a podcast, read, or watch some TV to help pass the time. Exercise to suit the seasons. In Australia that might be hot yoga in winter, swimming in summer, hiking and gardening in spring, and running in autumn.

How much exercise should you do? The Australian Department of Health and Human Services recommends that adults aged between 18 and 64 years should aim for at least 150 minutes of moderate aerobic activity or 75 minutes of vigorous activity over the course of the week. The general rule of thumb is no less than 30 minutes of moderate activity daily, with two days of strength training a week. If you have a weight-loss or specific fitness goal, you'll need to do more.

After you've identified your reason for exercising and chosen your physical activities (it doesn't just have to be one), you can take some steps to set yourself up for success:

- Get enough sleep. Motivation is harder when you are tired. Statistically, more people exercise in the mornings, and it makes good sense. Your energy is highest, and it helps clear your mind for the day. I lay out my exercise gear the night before, so all I need to do in the morning is put on the gear and go.
- Make a commitment to yourself. Put your exercise time in the diary. If something else comes up, move the

appointment to another time that same day. Build a fitness schedule into your routine.
- Don't overdo it too early. Be realistic. Start slowly and build from there. Overdoing it can lead to injury and setbacks. Plus, you don't want to add to your excuse pile, right?
- Use an app and follow a realistic program. You might need to start with a doctor's appointment to get an idea of your fitness level and find a good place to start.
- Set mini-goals and stretch goals: it's rewarding when we hit milestones. And it's important to see your progress in the beginning.
- Choose a social goal to work towards. Perhaps a fun run with friends, or a fundraising walk. These help remove the excuses.
- Set some SMART exercise goals and put them in your diary (see Resources).

✎ Health in Action

Answer the following in your Learning Journal:
1. How often do you exercise at the moment?
2. What do you like to do for exercise?
3. What gets in the way of exercising more often?
4. What are you willing to do to become a more active person?
5. What would a weekly exercise plan look like?
6. Who would you include as exercise partners?
7. How do you think you will feel when you are active?

Create a weekly exercise plan, putting each daily exercise in your calendar as a repeat event.

Connection time

Connecting with others or with the natural world around us is vital for a healthy mind (something I talked about in the Relationship Anchor). It generates a positive feedback loop of social, emotional and physical wellbeing. We are social beings. When we are not being social, loneliness and isolation creep in, and when they stay, despair and depression arrive. Strong connections help us to feel happy, secure and supported. They contribute to our sense of purpose.

In the workplace, healthy connections and positive relationships are a sign that the business has a good culture and will be able to weather sudden changes. When relationships are solid at work, information is more easily exchanged, trust is higher and communication is clearer, enabling complex concepts to be understood more easily and workflow to be more productive.

> ### ✎ Health in Action
> Where might you find opportunities to do the following? Record your answers in your Learning Journal:
> - List your current relationships – a bit like an audit. Highlight your top 12. You can do this for work and home life.
> - Of your key relationships, do they nurture and nourish you? Give each one a score out of 10. If lower than 7, what can you do to strengthen/enhance these relationships?
> - Try to form new connections through hobbies, volunteer groups, sports and social events.
>
> Be open to new experiences. Try stepping out of your comfort zone and into the challenge zone – this is when life gets both interesting and worthwhile.

Play

We don't stop playing because we grow old;
we grow old because we stop playing.
—George Bernard Shaw

According to Dr Stuart Brown (2009), 'Play is an ancient, voluntary, inherently pleasurable, apparently purposeless activity or process that is undertaken for its own sake and that strengthens our muscles and our social skills, fertilizes brain activity, tempers and deepens our emotions, takes us out of time, and enables a state of balance and poise.'

We know that children gravitate to play and through this they learn new skills and abilities to tackle everyday challenges. But for some reason, as adults, we stop playing. Maybe we should stop thinking of play as child's play and look at it as a different way to learn new skills. It might also remind us that it's okay to have fun while we learn something. Play is a catalyst for experiencing more joy, creativity and innovation. It stimulates our imagination, helping us to adapt and problem-solve. We learn better when we are relaxed and having fun. Play distracts us from our worries and stresses, giving our brains a chance become more objective. It's another great way to trigger the release of endorphins, which boost pleasure and reduce pain (Cafasso, 2017). You can play on your own but playing with others is different. It gives us the opportunity to share laughter and fun, connect to others and the world around us. It builds empathy, compassion, trust and intimacy (Robinson et al., 2021).

You might have forgotten how to play. At some point as adults, play just seems to disappear off the radar, but we need to consciously bring it back. Throw judgement out the window and give ourselves permission to just be ourselves. That means turning off our devices and eliminating the distractions of our adult lives. Play can be active or quiet, inside or outside, alone or with others. Here are some tips to help you find fun in your day:

- Remember to look for opportunities to smile and laugh throughout the day (gratitude helps).
- Try something new – you can plan it or be spontaneous. Walk a new route for your exercise, take a bus to the end of the line and see where you end up, learn how to juggle.
- Watch what kids do. Play comes naturally to them. Walk down the street avoiding the cracks.
- Join up and join in. Sign up for social sport, start an art class, learn to dance or just dance badly in your lounge room.
- Turn up the volume and sing along – in the car, in the shower, while you're cooking dinner. Sing like you're on stage.
- If you have kids in your life, spend time with them. Learn from them.

✎ Health in Action

Take some time out to think of where you might find opportunities to play. Record your ideas in your Learning Journal.
1. What does being fun and playful mean to you?
2. How can you adopt a playful, joyful, positive attitude? Describe what it might look like.
3. Schedule a regular fun appointment in your diary.
4. When are you most likely to daydream? Allow yourself some daydream time in your day.

From the ideas in this section, make a commitment to do one or two of these regularly.

Flow and focus

Flow is being completely involved in an activity for its own sake. The ego falls away. Time flies. Every action, movement, and thought follows inevitably from the previous one.
—Mihaly Csikszentmihalyi

According to Csikszentmihalyi, the psychologist who recognised and named the concept of 'flow', we need to challenge ourselves daily with tasks that require a high degree of skill and commitment. He calls it 'complete engagement'. Flow is deeply satisfying: our mind is fully occupied and our attention is focused and directed on what is important. It is not possible to be in flow and stressed at the same time.

Flow quietens the inner critic so we can explore and create. It allows us to accomplish things that are both a stretch, worthwhile and, from an evolutionary perspective, may even be lifesaving. Flow feels effortless. Intense concentration changes our brains from the fast-moving beta wave of waking consciousness down to the far slower function between alpha and theta. Alpha is daydreaming mode when we slip from idea to idea without much internal resistance. Theta, on the other hand, only shows up during REM or just before we fall asleep, where ideas combine in new and innovative ways.

Flow boosts our performance across all areas of our lives. With it, we get better results, and faster, at home and in the workplace. The good news is, anyone can achieve flow, but it does take planning and structure. Here are some tips:

1. Create a list of clear goals list for the day. Include everything from writing a proposal to hanging out the washing. This will help with focus. Clear goals help lower your cognitive load.

2. Start your day with the most challenging tasks. Clear the decks of all other distractions – phone, watch, notifications. You will need a block of at least 90 minutes concentration time. The sweet spot ranges from 90 to 120 minutes. It's no coincidence that our REM cycle also runs at around 90 minutes.
3. Pick one of your strengths to apply during this period. If you can't think of any, check back in your Learning Journal for the strengths exercise in the Self-Awareness Anchor.
4. Schedule time for gratitude and mindfulness. They both encourage your attention to the present moment, which is where innovation, concentration and creativity occur.
5. At the end of each day, check your accomplishments off your list. It feels good and can help you relax at the end of the day.

Using your strengths is an important part of flow. When I am in flow, my focus is clear and directed and I'm unaware of what is happening around me. When I play the piano, I am thoroughly absorbed and don't notice the time. This is flow.

Deliberate rest

> *The clever man may work smarter not harder, they say,*
> *but the creative man – the true aesthete – doesn't work at all.*
> —author unknown

We are so busy thinking about how to work better, we tend not to think about how to rest better. Productivity is judged by what people do at their desks, but there is a vital work/rest connection that has a significant impact on our creativity, productivity, learning, inspiration and innovation. There is something called 'awake rest' and it's critical for good work. We need deliberate rest, where we can recharge while still being mentally active. Deliberate rest gives our mind a chance to recover from the inputs of the day, to process new experiences and lessons by embedding them in our memory. Without further inputs, our non-conscious mind has space to keep working. How often do your best ideas come up when you are not working? Deliberate rest allows the time to explore ideas and find solutions.

Common sense tells us that if we spend 12 hours at a desk it can't all be productive. We've all had that feeling of being fuzzy-headed at our desk. This is a highly unproductive and extremely taxing state. A sustainable productive mode includes periods of intensity with intermittent periods of deliberate rest. When you relax it turns out that your brain doesn't really switch off: it keeps functioning and becomes very active in the background. It starts working on problems you've recently been trying to grapple with. This is the science behind why you have your best ideas in the shower.

You know what it's like trying to remember who was in that movie, and the name pops into your head while you're doing something completely unrelated. This is the Default Mode Network (DMN) part of your brain that continues to work on that original problem. When our brain is using its DMN we go into unstructured thinking, which allows time to recover from the overstimulation of attention, busyness and motivation. Some important mental processes kick in during this downtime. The brain makes sense of its new learnings, which may partially explain why high performers habitually form a daily routine of intense work punctuated by breaks and recovery. According to Jabr (2013) moments of downtime may even be necessary to maintain a sense of self, but it is a matter of balance. Too much DMN time can have debilitating effects on our sense of self.

The best type of deliberate rest is physically active. Hobbies, such as painting, gardening, sudoku and crossword puzzles, are another option. Winston Churchill took daily two-hour naps and was an avid painter. In painting, like politics, you need vision and strategy, which is probably why it appealed to Churchill. In contrast, Adolf Hitler stayed awake for days at a time and was a heavy user of cocaine, heroin and methamphetamine. Even though it was close, we all know who won World War II! Charles Darwin took morning and afternoon walks, a routine that helped him produce countless books. Churchill and Darwin organised their day around three to four really intense hours of work followed by a period of deliberate rest.

There are some great examples where organisations are supporting this idea of deliberate rest. Covid has fast-tracked changes to working hours: some organisations are shortening the workday to five or six hours, or the work week to four days, rather than five. Others are adjusting meeting quantity and lengths, from the traditional 60-minute default calendar invite where every man and his dog are meant to attend, to the 15-minute speed meeting. Others are setting aside 'offline' time during the day so people can focus solely on their work without interruption.

Building deliberate rest into your day will require rethinking some long-held ideas of productivity. Choose something you find satisfying but different from your day job. You're trying to utilise your skills and strengths differently. If you use your brain and knowledge in your role, it is important to incorporate deliberate rest into your daily schedule. If you don't have the freedom to restructure your day, you can still access active rest at home. I discovered during Covid lockdown that I enjoy working on a jigsaw puzzle in between clients and writing sessions. I incorporated 'puzzle time' on my daily whiteboard scheduler so that after periods of work, I could take a puzzle break.

Deliberate rest is a skill to learn. It needs to be consciously integrated into your routines, so that it becomes psychologically and physically restorative, but also mentally productive. Here are four things we can do to achieve deliberate rest (Pang, 2018):

1. Take rest seriously. The rest we get is the rest we take.
2. Recognise the value of boundaries. We live in a world where you can carry your office around in your pocket, and that's not always a good thing.

3. Have a hobby or exercise that competes with work. It will force you to leave work to meet those other commitments.
4. Try to do your active rest activity with other people. It holds you accountable to show up and makes it more enjoyable.

> ### ✎ Health in Action
> Answer the following questions in your Learning Journal:
> 1. Do you have any current hobbies or activities that fit the deliberate rest description?
> 2. List them – even ones you've not done for a long time.
> 3. What other deliberate rest activities could you commit to doing regularly?
> 4. Think about how you can integrate your deliberate rest activities into a daily practice.

Sleep

Knowing what we know about deliberate rest and downtime, it should come as no surprise that sleep is important! We need good sleep for our physical and mental health but it's easy to slip into bad sleeping habits, going to bed later and later each night. We are consumed and distracted at the wrong end of the day. It doesn't matter how well we look after our bodies during the day if we don't get enough sleep at night. If you are having trouble getting to sleep, staying asleep or functioning normally during the day it is important to see a doctor because there might be an underlying health problem.

According to the National Sleep Foundation, the sleep window for an adult is 7–9 hours each night. Teenagers need slightly more and older adults, slightly less. While we all have different sleep habits and requirements, there are sleep behaviours that help determine good quality sleep. These include:

- falling asleep within 30 minutes
- waking up no more than once during the night
- falling back asleep within 20 minutes of waking up during the night
- feeling refreshed when you get up
- feeling alert and able to concentrate during the day.

✎ Health in Action

Everyone's sleep needs are different and the questions below may help you find out yours. Write down the answers in your Learning Journal:

- On average, how much sleep do you feel you need to have a productive, healthy and happy day?
- In any week, how often do you get a full night's sleep?
- How much sleep do you (honestly) get most nights? – this may be very different from what you need.
- Do you feel fully awake half an hour from rising? (If the answer is no, then see if there's something you can do to give yourself a better night's sleep.
- What stops you from getting the sleep you need?
- Do you have any sleep problems? If so, is there something that could be done to help them? What might be stopping you?
- Do you depend on caffeine to get you through the day?
- Do you feel a slump in energy in the middle of the afternoon?

Now that you've done a sleep audit, take some time to address some of the issues raised here. It may be a simple 'stop caffeine by 3 pm', or visiting your GP to get some further advice, or setting an alarm to turn out your light at night.

If you are having trouble with sleep, there are some strategies and techniques to help. Try avoiding caffeine, too much alcohol and eating a late dinner. Get good exposure to natural light during the day to stimulate your natural circadian rhythm and the production of melatonin. If you are a daytime napper, keep it short. Get plenty of exercise, but not just before bedtime. Your bedroom is important – you need a good mattress and pillow and, ideally, the temperature should be on the cool side, somewhere between 15.6 and 19.4°C (Okamoto-Mizuno & Mizuno, 2012). If noise is a problem, listen to white noise, have a fan running or use earplugs. Essential oils have been used for centuries to promote relaxation thanks to the direct line between smell, emotions and memory. Lavender, vanilla, rose and geranium, jasmine, sandalwood and citrus are all great relaxation oils (Kim & Hur, 2016).

Getting to bed earlier and having a consistent pre-bed routine helps your body unwind. A routine will signal to your mind and body that it's time to get ready for sleep. It could include relaxation, meditation or writing in your gratitude journal. As much as possible try to disconnect from devices that produce the blue light that suppresses melatonin. Harvard Medical School tips for protecting yourself from blue light at night include:

- using dim red lights for night lights, as they are less likely to impact your circadian rhythm or suppress melatonin
- avoiding bright screens well before bed
- wearing blue-blocking glasses or installing an app that filters the blue/green wavelength in the evenings.

By simply adjusting and paying attention to how much sleep you get, your life will feel better. You will be able to think more clearly, have more energy, make better decisions, and generally be better company. If you'd like to know more about how to improve your sleep and health, there is valuable up-to-date health info and tools at sleepfoundation.org.

Anchor Self – Health

Take some time out to conduct your Health DIY Assessment.

Give yourself a score out of 10, where 10 is true all of the time and 1 is never true.

Health	1–10
I have a good understanding of my health	
Overall, I am physically fit and well	
I take good care of my physical health daily	
I always make healthy food choices	
I always get a good night's sleep (7–9 hours)	
When I feel flat, I look after myself well	
I use wellbeing strategies to keep my mind healthy	
I have balance in my day	
Health TOTAL	

When you have added up your score, out of a total of 80, colour in your Health Anchor score on the circumplex. Use the Scoring Key as your guide. As you progress through this book, you can return to your assessment and continue to colour in the various Anchors.*

---

* At the end of the book, your individual Anchor scores can be translated across to form your Anchor Self-profile.

HEALTH

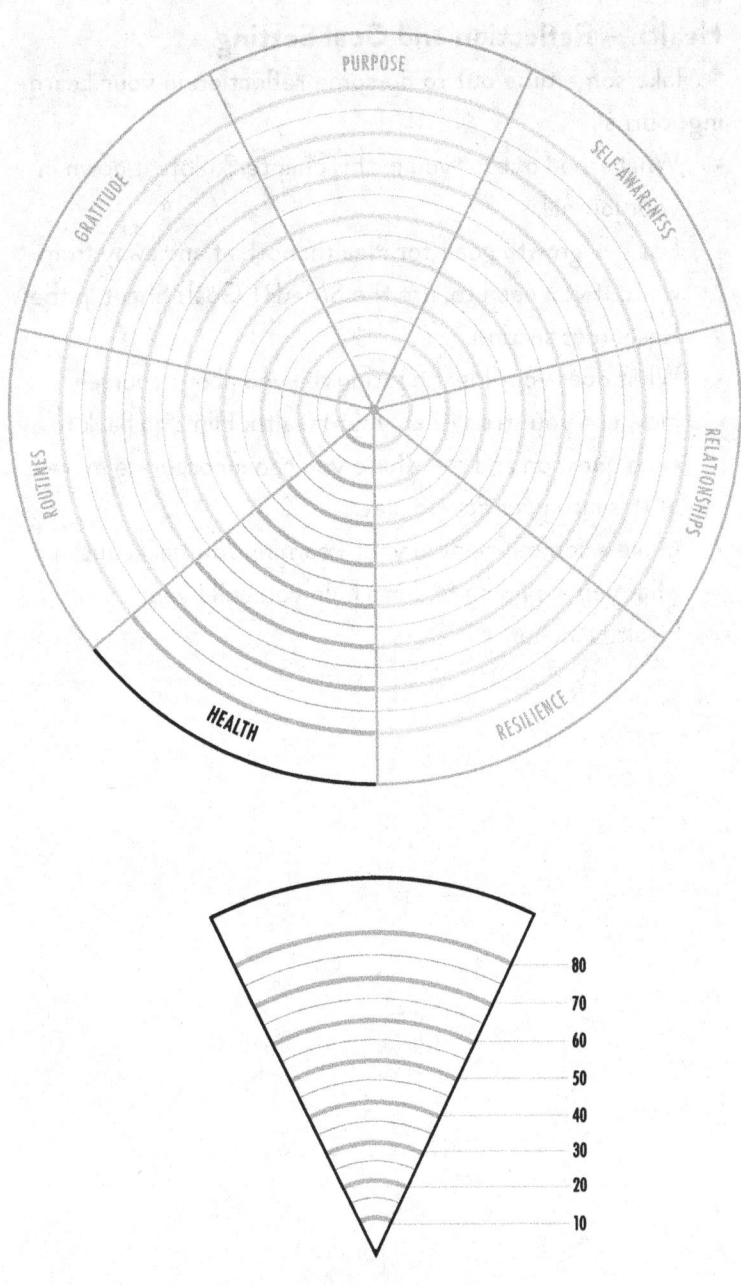

Scoring Key

Health – Reflection and Goal Setting

✎ Take some time out to do some reflection in your Learning Journal.

- What stood out for you in this chapter? Note it down in your journal.
- List two growth goals for Health, both at and away from work. If you need to, use the SMART Goals Sheet in the Resources section.
- What does your Health rating tell you about yourself?
- How can you strengthen your Health. Hint: go back to each question and see where you can incorporate more of this into your day-to-day.
- Make a commitment in your Learning Journal about what you are going to do to help you build your Health Anchor.

10

Routines

We are what we repeatedly do. Excellence, then, is not an act, but a habit.

—Aristotle

One of the fundamentals of living and leading well is being able to get stuff done. It gives us a sense of empowerment and achievement. This anchor shows us what we need to be mindful of in order to achieve things. This chapter covers the importance and benefits of having routines, as well as the significance of our habits. Get ready to read about time management, procrastination, fragmented attention and managing white space.

Why is Routine important?

Knowing what comes next

A routine is a sequence of events or habits that you do repeatedly. The things you do that form the rhythm in your daily life. Waking up at 6.30 am, going for a run, showering, breakfasting and dressing each morning is a routine. Routines help us regulate our normal activities and free us from decision-making for small things. They give our brain time to devote to the trickier parts of our lives, such as being innovative, strategic and creative. An unclogged brain is more receptive to new ideas and having fun. Implementing a routine gives you a sense of control. In case you're wondering, it doesn't spell the end of spontaneity. There are many opportunities to feed in 'unscheduled time'.

The structure of a routine is comforting because it involves things we do well and offers us certainty when certainty might be hard to come by. When my daughter was particularly unwell, I made a point of making my bed nicely and tidying my bedroom every morning before getting on with the day (I still do). It gives me comfort in the chaos of everything, knowing that at least one room of the house is in order. Routines provide an anchor of predictability in our increasingly unpredictable lives. They allow us to carve out the time to pursue what's really important to us every single day. A number of famously gifted people, including Freud, William James, Beethoven and Georgia O'Keefe used routines to become successful and highly productive.

In a *Paris Review* interview, Haruki Murakami said: 'When I'm in writing mode for a novel, I get up at 4 am and work for five to six hours. In the afternoon, I run for ten kilometres or swim for 1,500 metres (or do both), then I read a bit and listen to some music. I go to bed at 9 pm. I keep to this routine every day without variation. The repetition itself becomes the important thing; it's a form of mesmerism. I mesmerise myself to reach a deeper state of mind.'

I'm not suggesting you need to be Murakami, but the key here is the regularity of a behaviour. You don't need to think about what you're going to be doing at a particular time of day. I should probably say that repetition doesn't necessarily make something valuable or effective. Some routines are not helpful. We need to be prepared to change a routine if it stops working for us. If you have kids, most routines need regular revising.

Routines benefit our stress levels, improve sleep and overall health, and set a positive example for others. Having an effective routine is not only a game-changer, but a key anchor, enabling you to live and lead a great life. The trick is knowing what's important and what is not. If your values are embedded in your routines, you will stay on track to fulfil your goals.

You get the idea. Having a routine is good; not having a routine is not so good. Living and leading a great life demands proper nutrition, good sleep hygiene, as well as regular exercise and being effective at work. When we live without routine, sleep, productivity and health suffer. The constant background worry about uncompleted tasks causes stress. Sleeping, eating well and exercising require advance planning. When we don't have a nightly bed routine or time for sleeping, our bodies miss the necessary sleep. When we don't plan our meals or have the essential groceries, high fat and sugar substitutes are just a click away.

What the research says

Mason Currey, author of *The Daily Rituals*, researched the day-to-day routines of great artists. He found that, 'In the right hands, [a routine] can be a finely calibrated mechanism for taking advantage of a range of limited resources: time (the most limited resource of all) as well as willpower, self-discipline, optimism. A solid routine fosters a well-worn groove for one's mental energies and helps stave off the tyranny of moods.'

The Prince's Trust Youth Index in 2012 found that an absence of a daily routine, such as regular bedtimes and set mealtimes, impacts on a young person's school grades, general wellbeing and future prospects. The report also found a strong correlation between those who 'lacked structure and direction' while growing with a low index of contentment compared to their peers.

In 1938 Lithuanian psychologist Bluma Zeigarnik observed that our brain wants to resolve unfinished tasks, and that we will retain the task in our memories until resolved. In those quieter times of 'not working' our brains go about their business attempting to complete them, enabling the process of forgetting to take place (1938). This phenomenon is now referred to as the Zeigarnik effect. Under some circumstances (Wilson & Schooler, 1991), conscious thought deteriorates the quality of our decisions, but when we think unconsciously, in the midst of a routine or doing something other than 'trying to think', we have been found to perform significantly better. It seems that our unconscious processes have the capacity to work on different things in parallel and can integrate a large amount of information to solve problems in more sophisticated ways (Dijksterhuis et al., 2006).

If routines are the solid, reliable tower, then habits are the building blocks. James Clear, author of *Atomic Habits* (2018), explains that the process of habit formation begins with trial and error. He says that whenever we come across a new situation in our life, our brains have to make a decision on how to respond. The first time you come across a problem you're not entirely sure of how to solve it. Neurological activity in your brain is high, you are taking in a lot of new information and trying to make sense of it all while your brain is busy learning the most effective course of action. In time we stumble across a solution and receive an unexpected reward. Your brain immediately takes note of the events that led to that reward because it is constantly looking for ways to save effort. The next time that situation or problem presents itself, your brain will seek that reward again. Over time we refine the behaviour so that we can get to the reward more easily and the useful actions get reinforced. That is habit forming.

From our brain's perspective, when it learns that a certain action or cue is associated with a reward, dopamine neurons learn to fire whenever the cue appears, even before the reward is given. Dopamine does more than simply reward you: it motivates you to seek the pleasure again. And that's how a habit is so easily formed. As soon as you see the cue, your brain begins to anticipate the reward. Anticipation is part of the pleasure.

It's possible that routines can help us deal with the growing number of distractions we face each day. Phones are an immense distraction. I know mine is. Some reports suggest that people check their phones approximately every 12 minutes while awake, with 71% never turning their phone off and 40% checking almost as soon as they wake (Ofcom, 2018). Covid and working from home has only exacerbated this (Zalani, 2021). Similarly, always being 'on', but not giving our full attention to anything is equally destructive, creating a constant state of ineffective alertness. It has been coined Continuous Partial Attention or CPA, where we are constantly scanning the world in a hyper-alert state, but never with full attention. The long-term impact giving rise to our stress hormones adrenaline and cortisol.

The Routine Toolkit

Topics covered:
- dealing with change
- flexible routines
- creating a routine
- habits
- changing habits
- finding time
- procrastination
- managing interruptions
- making your calendar work for you.

We often do our best thinking when we are not thinking, and this is the beauty of the routine. Our routine sets up a relaxed state. The flow of blood increases around our body, giving us more energy, and our minds become calm and clear because there is no stress. Our brain keeps ticking along processing information and helping us come up with answers. Moreover, our brains do not like unfinished tasks because they inhibit our ability to forget, so it looks for opportunities to 'solve' them. We tend to remember unfinished tasks better in the 'non-thinking' state. Which explains why that unfinished presentation pops into your mind when you're in the shower. TV dramas take advantage of this by ending an episode with an unfinished story arc; you want to keep watching it until it's complete. By building a routine, you allow your brain to do its best thinking. If you start working towards a goal and don't finish it, trust that your brain will keep working on it while you set about your daily routine.

> **✎ Routines in Action**
> Answer the following questions in your Learning Journal:
> 1. When do you do your best thinking?
> 2. What are some of your routines?
> 3. Which ones serve you?
> 4. Which ones hinder?

Dealing with change

During the early days of Covid lockdown, many people working from home didn't have the usual work commute, daily work preparation, or their water-cooler conversations. It gave us up to 3–4 hours extra in our day. We won some time back, but our usual routines became redundant. What happened next was really interesting: some floundered, others maintained business as usual, and some thrived. The difference I saw was in how they approached their day.

Some abandoned their daily routines, embracing erratic mealtimes, crazy work schedules, with limited or no exercise and unsatisfactory sleep schedules. Many people resisted building a new routine as they waited for a 'return to normal'. Even my high-functioning clients, colleagues and friends, who were used to getting through significant amounts of work in their day, claimed to be unproductive and exhausted. Not all of them realised they'd lost their routines. Those that were more attuned, adaptive and exploratory pivoted rapidly to find new routines to fit the circumstances. They coped more easily and continued with a productive workflow.

Change is not unique to Covid-19. Life can throw anything at us. When we embrace change, it is easier to manage. When we are willing to look for better ways of being, doing, thinking and managing (ourselves and others), and find ways to routinise them we give ourselves the opportunity for growth and continual improvement. Given that change is the only constant, our routines need to be flexible. It might sound counter-intuitive, but we need structure in order to adapt. It helps contain and control the chaos of everyday life. Like this:

Seek Improvement opportunities/refinements (being–doing–managing–thinking) → *Implement changes* → *Routinise Changes* → *Search for Improvement opportunities/refinements* → *etc.*

Flexible routines

A routine that is too strict might see us miss out on the world around us. It can prevent us from engaging with the world. We need to think flexibly and have flexible routines and habits because sh!t happens and we need to pivot in line with our circumstances. If our routines are impacting negatively on those around us, we need to be willing to 'let go' for a bit. You might, for example, have a very rigid exercise and meal plan, but decide to go away with a group of friends. Sticking to your routine will most likely impact your enjoyment and connection with your friends. We also need to try new things to discover opportunities to improve what and how we do things. If we never question, we won't grow and develop.

Without flexibility it is almost impossible to appropriately engage with the world. Sometimes your routine will serve you, other times it will inhibit. Bear in mind that the most common reason to adjust your routine will be to support your relationships. To remain flexible look at the patterns of behaviour that have become routinised and question their service to you. Do they take up too much mind-numbing time? Are they enabling you to avoid something new? Once you have a good idea of the routines you have established in your life, you can review them. Even small changes can have a big impact on how you think, perform and engage with the world.

Creating a Routine

At the start of his day, Benjamin Franklin asked, 'What good shall I do this day?' and in the evening he asked, 'What good have I done today?' There are two parts to creating a valuable routine: choosing what should be in it and setting it up for success.

You want your routine to include the most important must-haves in your day. You will need a checklist and a timing schedule for the various parts of your day. Everyone's routines will be different. Your working weekday routine will be different from your weekend routine. That cherished lazy, slow Sunday morning sleep-in, followed by a cooked breakfast and long slow run or walk after reading the news is also a routine. The start and the end of the day are important bookends for your daily routine.

A consistent morning routine will prepare you for the day's challenges. It might include waking at the same, making your bed, meditating, setting a daily intention, having a coffee, going for a run, meeting a friend for a morning walk, walking the dogs, having a shower, making and eating breakfast.

A solid evening routine will help you clear your mind ready for a good night's sleep. Pre-bedtime activities set you up for the rest of your evening. Doing an activity to clear your mind such as meditation or reading an enjoyable book or watching an easy TV series are some ideas. Perhaps tidying up calms your mind and gets you ready for the next day. Taking 20 minutes each evening to tidy helps keep the order in your house and gives you a chance to reflect on your wins for the day. Your pre-bedtime routine would likely finish with going to the loo then brushing your teeth. Finally, once in bed you might like to check or change your morning alarm, read for a while, write in your gratitude journal or do a sleep meditation.

Here are some of the things my clients include in their routines:

- **Meditation**: 10–15 minutes of meditation before getting out of bed in the mornings is a great way to set you up for the day and to bring you into the here and now. In the evening, before sleeping, you may choose a relaxing gratitude meditation.
- **Create a daily intention**: An attitude or value you wish to adopt for the day. Some of the intentions I have used include: relax, practise courage, focus and patience, and contribute. I then write this on the top of my whiteboard in the morning.

- **Active rest activities**: You will have already read that mine are playing piano, cooking and doing jigsaw puzzles. What are yours? To remind you, look back in your Learning Journal. Schedule these to give your mind a rest and add some variety in your day (check back in with your Health Anchor to jog your memory).
- **Exercise**: Lock it in the diary, make it happen. Even when you don't feel like it. Schedule time for a run, a walk with the dog, some friends, your kids, ride a bike, go for a swim, do a gym session. Each day may be different, but if it's in your routine you're more likely to keep it up.
- **Meals**: There is no doubt that skipping meals such as breakfast or lunch has an impact on how we function. Try having breakfast, lunch, some afternoon tea and dinner at around about the same time each day. It will help your brain function and regulate your metabolism.
- **Family time**: Quality time with our families and the ones we love is incredibly important. As crazy as this sounds, if we don't schedule time to spend with them, those precious hours can get eaten up with the other 'shoulds' in life.
- **Friends time**: Make time for regular catch-ups with friends. It's important to keep these connections strong. I lock in a standing Saturday breakfast with a girlfriend. It's great, because we are both very busy but we make it happen and it's so rewarding. If you can't connect in person, create a chat group. Or you could try ticking two boxes at once and exercise with a friend.

Workday planning time

Plan to plan. Allow time to create your to-do list for the day. Note when you have regular meetings and include them in your planning. Prioritise everything that needs to be done for the day. As part of my daily routine, I make good use of a whiteboard. Each morning, I clean it off from the day before, noting the things that need to carry over into that day. I write the day and date at the top: and then on the right-hand side I bullet-point everything that I hope to do for the day. The list is extensive and includes household chores, my piano practice, along with the exercise I'm committing to do for the day. I write down all of my locked-in work commitments (scheduled client meetings, coaching sessions, etc).

On the left side of the whiteboard, I make a timeline, starting at whatever time I think I'll get to my desk through to the end of the day, marking in all the known appointments and break times. I then pepper the rest of the to-do list in the gaps. Lastly, after seeing what I have on for the day I set an intention or a value that I want to adopt to see me get through the day. I write that up the top. I also put in a log of my water/coffee/tea intake so I can be mindful of what I am having. When everything is captured on this whiteboard, I feel comforted, knowing that I don't have to remember what's next. This leaves room for me to focus on what I really need to think about for that part of the day.

Workday thinking time

Without a doubt, we all need some thinking time to reflect and problem solve. All of my successful clients do this. Dedication to thinking time once or twice a week is a minimum. Booking in time every month with a colleague, mentor or coach enables you to review where you're at, what is going well and not well. I was working with a client only this week who was not getting any thinking time. It wasn't in the diary and her time was being eaten up with various meetings and other interruptions. She did tell me, though, that when time was blocked out in her diary, meetings were generally organised around that time. So, after agreeing that she wanted three hours a week thinking time, she chose Wednesday afternoons as it's a working-from-home day with fewer interruptions. She agreed that if that time was encroached on, she would move it to another part of her week.

Work time

Strike a balance between time with others and time you need working alone. It helps to break down your week into the roles you need to fulfil, then work out how much time you should spend on each role. Try thinking of your schedule in fortnight blocks, and use a traffic light system to prioritise tasks. Red light means you need to stop what you're doing and address the issue right away. A yellow light is a task that may seem urgent, but isn't that important. Often these tasks can be put aside without any detrimental effect on your day and should be treated as such. A green light priority is not particularly time sensitive. Green light priorities often get lost in the day-to-day rush of to-dos because while they are important, they don't have that sense of urgency. Categorising your tasks will help you to prioritise your time more effectively and ensure that you only work where you need to.

Workday breaks

You will need breaks. Make them happen. They are critical to keep a clear head and give your eyes a break. If you can, find some outside or 'green time' (look up at the blue sky, walk on the grass, notice the bird life). Set up walk-and-talk meetings with a couple of colleagues, where possible, or while you're on the phone. A healthy lunchbreak away from your desk is very important and again, all too often missed. Don't worry, your mind will still be working and problem solving in the background.

Building a new routine takes commitment and discipline. It's like any type of training: the more you do it the easier it becomes. The good news is that your brain is busily building new neural pathways to help you out. You can use tips and ideas from others, but essentially your routine is yours to build and yours to own.

> 📎 **Routines in Action**
>
> Take some time out in your Learning Journal to review your routines.
>
> 1. Flip back through your journal to the Values exercise in the Self-Awareness Anchor.
> 2. Remember, you should have a good rationale for everything in your routine.
> 3. Go through your day. See if you can identify the routines that are working for you, and those that could do with some reviewing.
> 4. Set aside some routine planning time with a whiteboard or some large notepaper.
> 5. Note down the goals and projects you are working on and their timelines. Some goals can be combined, for example, exercise + kids and/or relationships.
> 6. Break each goal down into smaller achievable components that can be inserted into your diary.
> 7. Plan your day, week and fortnight in line with your 7 roles (refer back to your Self-Awareness Anchor).
>
> Remember to book in time to review your routine. Check that it's working for you. Make tweaks if you need.

Understanding habits

We are what we do. Excellence, therefore, is not an act, but a habit.

—Aristotle

Imagine having to think about how to clean your teeth every single time you did it. Luckily cleaning your teeth is a habit, one of those unconscious actions we do automatically. They develop over time and form when our brain turns a sequence of actions into an automatic behaviour. Routines are a collection of habits. As with routines, habits help make our lives efficient. According to Charles Duhigg (2014), about 40–45% of what we do every day is habituated. If we are going to be doing things without awareness, we should probably make sure they are positive things!

Habits create efficiencies and exist so we can think about doing what's important. When a behaviour becomes automatic, it moves into the basal ganglia, which is one of the oldest structures in our brain. When things happen in the basal ganglia, it doesn't feel like thought or a decision. So, if you spend eight hours a day at work, 40% of that will translate to roughly three and a half of those hours being done automatically, without thought, filtering or decisions and, importantly, without stress. Decisions, by their very nature are stressful. So by reducing the number of decisions, you reduce the amount of stress. When a habit emerges, the brain stops fully participating in the decision-making, and this has advantages and disadvantages. Think about the first time you made your way to your current workplace. You would have researched the ways to get there, planned your route, even the shoes you'd need to wear if a lot of walking was involved and so on. But after a while it happens on autopilot. Sometimes you don't even realise how you got to where you were going.

The challenge with habits lies at the heart of their usefulness – we're not aware of them! Some of your habits might be past their 'use by' date. They either need to go or could simply do with a 'tune-up'. If they are good habits – fantastic. If they are bad habits, we have to work hard to replace them. And we do this by bringing them to the surface and becoming aware of them. With conscious awareness we can objectively determine if the habit still serves us. To do this we sometimes need the help of others.

Many years ago, I decided to quit smoking. At the time I was a heavy smoker but knew it wasn't good for me. I put the half-empty packet of cigarettes in the cutlery drawer and decided that was the moment to stop smoking. I rang Quitline and they helped me understand my smoking habits and triggers. Until that conversation I hadn't been consciously aware of them. They suggested I find an 'innocuous replacement behaviour' that I could do each time I was triggered by the cue to smoke. It was then I learned that you can't break a habit: you need to replace it with something else. I used two replacement behaviours. Every time I felt like a cigarette, I'd either have a glass of water or a piece of gum. I knew that the nicotine would be out of my system within about 24–48 hours and after that, all I'd have to cope with was breaking the physical habit of smoking. Funny thing is, to this day, all these years later, I still have a piece of gum when I get in the car! I probably started smoking to be rebellious. I had a very solid reason to stop and no longer needed to be a rebel. Whenever I felt tempted to have a cigarette, I thought about this rationale to help me.

A quick word about addiction. Addiction can look like a habit. It involves regular behaviours and is often done on autopilot, but addiction is far more complex. By definition, addictions always have negative consequences on your health, finances, relationships or self-esteem. So, thankfully, my morning coffee is just a lovely enjoyable habit. In Australia the four most common addictions are alcohol, smoking, illicit drugs and gambling. There are now addictions to mobile phones and other online applications such as gaming and pornography. I won't explore addiction in this book, but it's important to make the distinction between habit and addiction. If you do want to lead a really great life and you're aware that you have an addiction, addressing it will offer huge benefits. First acknowledge the problem, then seek help from a professional.

Changing habits

Habits never truly disappear. We just change or replace them. With work and effort we can change a habit to be more in line with who we want and need to be (Duhigg, 2014). There is no simple formula: giving up smoking is different from changing how you speak to your partner, which is different again from how you approach your inbox at work. The better you understand yourself (remember the all-important Self-Awareness Anchor), the easier it will be for you to understand the origin and the motivation behind the habit. It gives you the chance to question its efficacy. You are the only person who can do that. We can all change our habits and create new ones, but it is hard. It takes self-awareness along with a very good rationale. We often hear that it takes 21 days to form a new habit. In actual fact, it's the number of times an action takes place that impacts habit formation, rather than the time.

To live and lead a great life, you don't necessarily have to change big things. Changing a few smaller habits can make a big difference. Research has shown us that habits never truly disappear. They are just overpowered by other habits. Cravings are the brain's motivator. For something to become a habit, our brain must crave it. If you don't have a very good reason to change a habit, you won't. Studies show that once you have this reason to change and are aware of the cue or prompt of a particular habit, it becomes easier to notice it, think about it and change it. This rationale can help you shift your behaviour from non-conscious to conscious. Once you choose a positive replacement behaviour, you start making small adjustments to your day that over a year, or a decade, can add up to a huge difference.

In James Clear's book *Atomic Habits* he talks about habit-stacking. It is the process of integrating some form of new process to an already existing routine to fast-track its formation as a new habit. Basically, you are connecting a new habit to an existing routine. You often decide what to do next based on what you've just finished doing. When you do this often enough, you are stacking habits. For example, going to the bathroom, leads to washing and drying hands, which reminds us that we need to put the dirty towels in the laundry, so we add the laundry detergent to the shopping list, and so on. Each action triggers the next behaviour.

You can live and lead a better life by consciously crafting and refining your habits to become useful and healthy ones. Start to raise your awareness by making a list of your daily habits and then determine if they are serving you or detracting from who it is you want to be. Here are a few tips before you start your habit activity:

- If you want to incorporate a difficult behaviour, do something you enjoy just beforehand (to give yourself some endorphins).
- Pair your new habit with something you already enjoy doing. Make it attractive. This is about opportunities to habit-stack.
- Keep it real. Know what you can and can't do. If you're not sure, ask someone who will be honest with you.

> ✎ **Routines in Action**
> Go through these steps and record them in your Learning Journal to replace an old habit with a new habit.
> 1. Determine the current habit you want to change.
> 2. Create a solid rationale for the change. This may involve exploring where the behaviour originated in your own personal history.
> 3. Choose the replacement behaviour.
> 4. See where you can fit that into your daily routine.
> 5. Habit-stack it on to another existing habit and go for it.
> 6. Be patient: give the replacement habit time to form.
> 7. Be kind to yourself, there may be some missteps along the way.

Finding time

Don't count every hour in the day,
make every hour in the day count.
—author unknown

We all have exactly the same amount of time in the day. High performers aren't given a special extra hour. When we don't make the most of our time, we don't finish things. I used to joke that washing the dog was always number ten on my to-do list. Unsurprisingly, it never got done! If I had scheduled a dog wash on the first Saturday morning of each month, there was a far better chance we would have a clean dog. We all have the same amount of time: the difference is how we use it. If you live to 90 years of age, you'll have 4680 weeks in your life (see p. 198). Might sound like a lot, but if you're around 37 years of age, you've used 1924 of those weeks already, leaving you only 2756 weeks left! Remember, the last few years of your life aren't all that productive. With all excuses aside, there aren't that many weeks left for you to do what you need to do!

My clients tell me about how busy they are, and all the meetings they must attend, all the work that needs to be done. Then they go on to say that they sometimes have no idea why they're in a particular meeting. Sound familiar? If you don't know why you're there, or anywhere else for that matter, then find out. Maybe you don't need to be there! You're probably going to be more effective somewhere else. Now that you know the clock is ticking, perhaps you will start to use your time more diligently.

I had one client who was so swamped with work he wasn't getting to his own important work. When we looked at the structure of his week, we could see that he met with eight of his direct reports every single week on a Monday. Each person had one whole hour! That was a full 8-hour day or 20% of his work already accounted for in his week. These meetings, though, were an important part of guiding them to work independently for the rest of the week. So, he agreed to cut each meeting back by 20 minutes and incorporated each with an agenda. To help him stay on time, he stacked two meetings back-to-back, gaining 40 minutes of his own time for each two-hour block. His new schedule gave him breaks where he was able to get a good chunk of his own work done and fit in a luxurious one-hour lunch. In all, from this small adjustment he regained 220 minutes. His staff also got the benefit of the extra time to put towards their own reflection, planning and consolidating. That's a win-win.

7 ANCHORS

Time in 4680 weeks or 90 years

> ### ✎ Routines in Action
> Think about how you spend the time in your life and do the following in your Learning Journal:
> 1. Cross off how many weeks you've used up in the graphic on p. 198 to see just how many weeks you will have left if you live until 90 years of age (halfway is 45 years).
> 2. What does this mean to you?
> 3. How might you start to use your time more effectively?
> 4. Where do you see inefficiencies?
> 5. Where do you see indulgences that ultimately aren't serving you?
> 6. What can you commit to doing differently as a result of the above exercise?

Procrastination

One of the challenges in managing our time is procrastination. Have you ever sat down at your computer with good intentions to work on that submission but end up down a Google rabbit-hole? We all find ourselves doing other things when we're supposed to be doing something else. The Cambridge Dictionary defines procrastination as, 'To keep delaying something that must be done, often because it is unpleasant or boring.' So why don't we just get on and do what we're avoiding then?! It's not that easy. Procrastination is not just about poor time management. The difference between poor time managers and procrastinators, is that procrastinators carry accompanying feelings of guilt, shame, or anxiety with their decision to delay. Professor Joseph Ferrari found that as many as 20% of us may be chronic procrastinators. He says, 'while everybody may procrastinate, not everyone is a procrastinator.' True procrastination is a complicated failure of self-regulation where we know that we'll suffer as a result of not doing that task.

When we procrastinate, we seek pleasure and avoid pain. It's natural for us to avoid feeling uncomfortable or having negative emotions.

When we avoid unpleasant or difficult tasks we feel better in the short term. Problem is, the long term catches up with us. You can avoid the uncomfortable feeling in the short term, but you can't avoid it forever. You can avoid getting something wrong in the short term which feels like a safe haven, but eventually you will have to take the risk. You can kid yourself that you work better under pressure, leaving whatever it is to the last minute. But this is a risky and false incentive. The impact on careers can be devastating with consistently missed opportunities (Metin et al., 2018). Severe procrastination has been linked to increased levels of stress, anxiety, poor job performance, failed relationships, lack of sleep, loss of appetite, along with the accompanying unpleasant bad moods. Procrastinators are also more likely to put off important health check-ups and regular exercise.

When my clients tell me they want to change or stop a particular behaviour, we look for a replacement behaviour. The good news is that there are some great strategies to help you reduce how often and how long you procrastinate:

1. Acknowledge something that you procrastinate about but know you need to get on with.
2. Name why you want to do it, why is it important, and what are the consequences of not doing it.
3. Visualise and describe how you'll feel when it's done. This helps to manage negative emotions.
4. Choose the opportunity you've laid out for yourself and muster some courage to get on with it, knowing it may be tough but it will be worth it.
5. Set yourself up for success. Make the task achievable by breaking it down into small realistic steps.
6. What do you need to get it done – tasks, skills, actions?
7. When: how often and for how long?
8. Who are the people you need to achieve this?

9. Acknowledge the things you know that might get in the way of doing it.
10. Live the commitment. Notice the emotions coming up. Even say them out loud. But don't let them stop you.
11. Remind yourself why it's important.
12. Get cracking.

> **✎ Routines in Action**
> In your Learning Journal note down:
> - When are you most likely to procrastinate?
> - List down your favourite procrastination strategies.
>
> Use the strategy above to overcome your procrastination.

Managing interruptions

Knowing how to deal with interruptions is a big part of managing time. 'Got a minute?' is never a minute. According to a study by the University of California Irvine, it takes an average of 23 minutes and 15 seconds to get back to the deep focus you had on a task once you have been distracted (Mark et al., 2008). So, three interruptions end up being just over an hour and they can be a key barrier to managing your time effectively. There are any number of interruptions that may cross your path in a day: phone calls, messages, social media, notifications, news updates, listening to people chatting, your boss or a colleague.

All of these interruptions unexpectedly drag your attention away from what you were working on. They rob you of your ability to be effective. The impact of this fragments your attention. Being distracted, where your attention is only required for a very short snippet, is the opposite to being in flow. Platforms like Facebook, Twitter, Instagram and TikTok are deliberately designed to be both addictive and to fragment your attention. If you spend large amounts of your day 'taking a quick look', research now shows that you can permanently reduce your capacity to apply the deep effort required to thrive (Newport, 2016). It might feel like we are multi-tasking, but we know from prefrontal cortex research that we do not have the capacity to multi-task. Instead, we are switching rapidly from task to task, usually doing neither well. Adrenaline and cortisol are designed to support us through bursts of intense activity, but in the long term cortisol can knock out the feel-good hormones, serotonin and dopamine. This affects our sleep and heart rate, leading us to feel on edge.

Essentially, life is more easeful, less stressful and we are more effective when we concentrate on one thing without interruptions. Part of overcoming our distractions is being aware of them and then implementing steps towards changing our behaviours to minimise them. Being more disciplined in our device use, eliminating distractions and managing how and when we interact with others will see us concentrate for longer, be more productive and feel a whole lot better.

The Five More Rule: an easy way to improve your concentration is by simply encouraging yourself to do five more of whatever it is that you're doing to extend your focus and build concentration. It might be five more minutes, five more exercises, five more pages.

✎ Routines in Action

Answer the following questions in your Learning Journal:

1. What devices/platforms interrupt your attention throughout your day? (Phone, email, apps – WhatsApp, Twitter, Facebook, Instagram.)
    a. Are there one or two or more you could honestly do without?
    b. What are you willing to switch off for certain parts of your day so that you can concentrate?
2. How often do you look at your phone?
    a. Do a self-assessment over one typical day. You can also look at your phone usage records.

> b. Use Do Not Disturb, Focus or Sleep modes to help avoid distractions
> 3. Are you willing to have some device-free zones in your house? The bathroom? The bedroom? The kitchen table?

Making your calendar work for you

If you don't have time to write down your goals, where are you going to find the time to accomplish them?

One of the things I teach my clients is to work their calendar really hard. Everything needs to go either into the diary or on that (whiteboard) to-do list. Calendars help with evaluating how long things take. When we review our daily schedule as the day progresses and again at the end of the day, we can learn how long things take to do and where we may have misjudged. With unfinished tasks written down we can roll them over to the next day. It's about having the routine and still being flexible enough to realise that we misjudge certain things. The better we get at it, the more realistically we can plan out our days.

Your goals are an essential part of your diary. They can essentially be broken down into two components: the goal outcome and the goal process. Your goal outcome is what you want to achieve, and your goal process is how you're going to get there. It's important to ensure that the 'process' part of your goal is scheduled into your diary. Wanting to run a half-marathon won't just happen unless you make time for it. The hours of dedication to training all need their place in your schedule. You may need to look at your sleep, especially as training ramps up closer to the event. Your diet might need adjustment. The terrain of the course will determine your training. A hilly course, a trail run, or a road race all have different requirements in different places. Where will you train? You might have to schedule in travel. Life becomes much simpler and accomplished when we work our calendar.

One of the forgotten parts of the daily timetable is something called 'white space'. It's the in-between time we all have peppered throughout our days and evenings. The time that doesn't make it in the diary, yet it adds up. Everyone has it. White space happens in between meetings or after finishing a piece of work/assignment and before starting the next thing. It can happen on your way to or from work. It can also happen after dinner. Without awareness of the in-between time, we risk wasting it. When you take the time to notice white space in your day, and use it constructively, you'll have much more time that you realise.

Think about how you spend your day. To be more effective you need to choose to be more effective. You have 96 x 15-minute blocks in a day. Every day! Approximately eight hours of your day is for sleeping, so you have 64 blocks left. In your day you also have to shower, get dressed, travel to/from work, have meals, go to meetings, do some work, etc. You also want to be fit, healthy, a good friend, a great mum/dad/son/daughter, be a great worker *and* have great relationships. *phew*! You can be good at *all* of these things if you dedicate quality time to each of them. Attending to some of those things doesn't always take a lot of time. And that's when white space comes in. If you use just 15 minutes of white space a day more effectively you will have 91 hours of effective time accumulated in one year! Imagine if every person you knew did that? What are you waiting for? Manage your white space to feel better and get more done.

'The secret of your future is hidden in your daily routine.'

—Mike Murdock

Anchor Self – Routines

Take some time out to conduct your Routines DIY Assessment.

Give yourself a score out of 10, where 10 is true all of the time and 1 is never true.

Routines	1–10
I get the most out of each day	
My day is planned	
I have balance in my day	
I am aware of the habits that don't serve me well	
I always focus on being more efficient	
I have clear boundaries between work and outside work	
I am always doing what I am meant to be doing	
I judge accurately how long something will take to do	
Routines TOTAL	

When you have added up your score, out of a total of 80, colour in your Routine Anchor score on the circumplex. Use the Scoring Key as your guide. As you progress through this book, you can return to your assessment and continue to colour in the various Anchors.[*]

---

[*] At the end of the book, your individual Anchor scores can be translated across to form your Anchor Self-profile.

ROUTINES

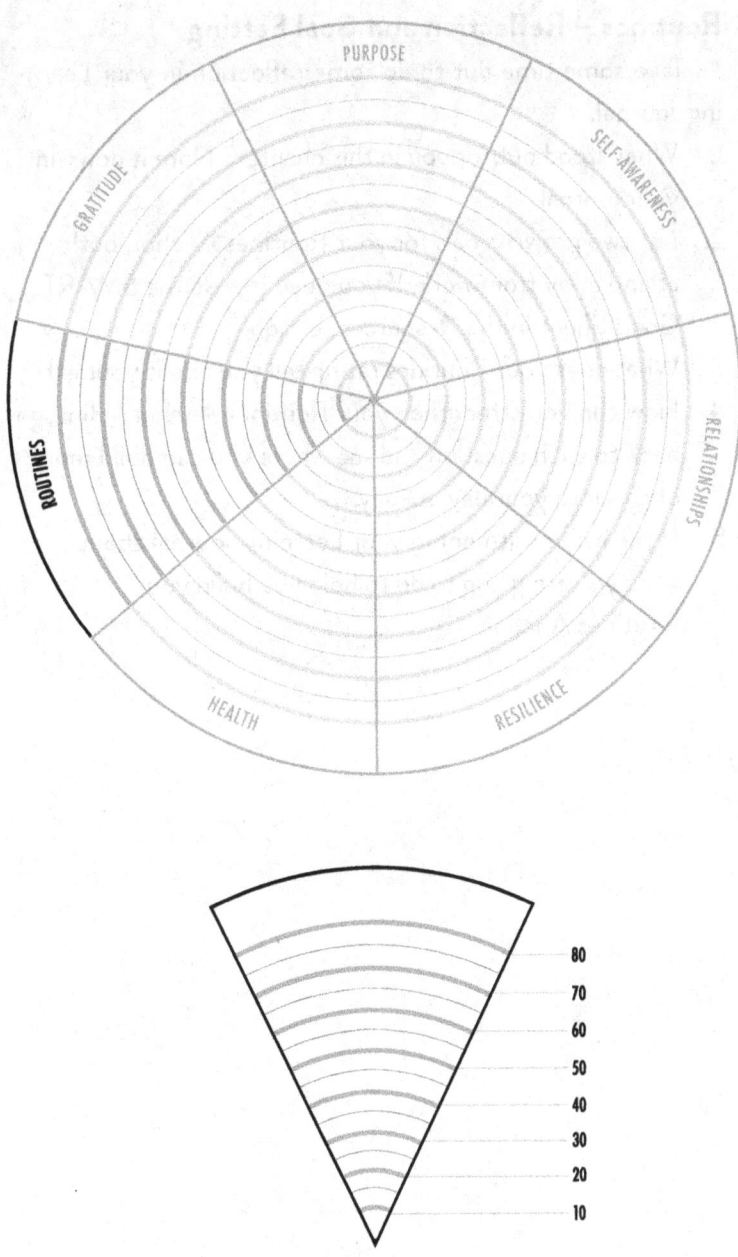

Scoring Key

Routines – Reflection and Goal Setting

✏️ Take some time out to do some reflection in your Learning Journal.
1. What stood out for you in this chapter? Note it down in your journal.
2. List two growth goals for your Routines Anchor, both at and away from work. If you need to, use the SMART Goals Sheet in the Resources section.
3. What does your Routines rating tell you about yourself?
4. How can you strengthen your Routines Anchor? Hint: go back to each question and see where you can build more of this into your day-to-day.
5. Make a commitment in your Learning Journal about what you are going to do to help you build your Routines Anchor.

11

Resilience

In this chapter I discuss what resilience is, how it works and why it matters. We will address how your attitudes impact your resilience and start to understand the importance of having a growth mindset. Building blocks for resilience, preventing burnout and the research that backs it up start to build a picture of how you can become more resilient.

What is Resilience?

Resilience refers to how well we respond to the pressures and demands of daily life. It's about understanding why we feel the way we do and our ability to develop strategies to deal with challenges more effectively. It is what gives people the psychological strength to cope with stress and hardship. Resilience is about how cognitively hardy we are. Facing change as a challenge, rather than perceived threat. Your level of resilience will affect how well you navigate through difficulty, along with your ability to recover.

Resilience is not about trying to carry on regardless of how we feel. Nor is it about being superhuman. It's about being able to carry on inclusive of how we feel, and taking that into consideration, so that we can manage ourselves as best as possible. The road to resilience is likely to involve considerable emotional distress. It's personal. It involves navigating well through our thoughts, feelings and situations. Anyone can develop it, but it does take time and effort.

In the workplace, Resilience is the defining characteristic of employees who deal well with the stresses and strains of an organisation. Resilient employees are regarded as more persistent, more actively engaged and report lower levels of work stress, regardless of workload. They deal with demands placed upon them especially when facing constantly changing priorities and heavy workloads.

Why is Resilience important?

Life is not about how fast you run or how high you climb but how well you bounce.

—Tigger, *Winnie the Pooh*

If something breaks, it doesn't mean we should give up on it or throw it away. When we face setbacks, find solutions and learn from our mistakes, we are stronger. The Japanese have a traditional art form known as Kintsugi, which has been described as the 'art of precious scars'. A precious metal is used, such as liquid gold, liquid silver or a lacquer dusted with powdered gold, to bring together the pieces of a broken pottery item and at the same time enhance the breaks. The pottery is not just given a new lease of life: it becomes even more refined thanks to its scars. When we look for ways to cope with challenging events in a positive way, we make room from the opportunity to learn. The cumulative effect of these experiences is the essence of resilience.

A Covid case study

One of my clients, who works for the state government, shared with me a talk he gave to his staff about his Covid-19 experience. The first thing he told the group was his frustration at people saying how wonderful things have been for them, when his lived experience was quite the opposite. He found things to be very difficult, as did many of his staff. He described his three phases of coping with Covid and the lockdown. The first phase he experienced was **Novelty**, where the first lockdown of six weeks felt temporary, even though it was uncomfortable. He, like many others, believed it was all going to pass. With that mindset the situation was just annoying and not ideal.

When the second lockdown occurred in Melbourne it endured for another four months but the end was not clearly defined for anyone. At this time, he entered what he called **Difficulty** and experienced disconnection. The reality of continuing to work at home at his kitchen bench was challenging and not ideal. If you're wondering why he chose his kitchen bench: it was only temporary, right? A form of grieving commenced as he realised relationships were more difficult to manage – both at work and at home. He felt disconnected and isolated. Boundaries blurred and work hours crept into personal time. There was no end in sight.

The third phase he called **Acceptance**, when he realised that the virus wasn't going away. There was no point fighting it. His attitude changed. He stopped resisting and started accepting the present situation as his reality. He stopped looking back and began to appreciate the now. He stopped being frustrated with his wife clanging around the house or the dog barking. After all, they had as much right to be there as he did! What was wonderful for me to hear was that the skills he used to navigate through this challenge all sit within the 7 Anchor Model, under which we had been working.

Relationships: Firstly, he realised he wasn't alone in this Covid imposition. It was a global issue. He felt an affinity with those around him. Indeed, there were many millions of people going through the same uncomfortable and distressing experience. Once he identified that he was lonely, he actively sought connection to others to discover their experiences. It helped him understand that everyone was in this together. Rather than isolate his experience, he found ways to connect with and help others, sometimes just by listening.

Gratitude: He wanted to keep things in perspective. He told the group, for example, that he was grateful to have a job when he knew many around him had lost theirs. He also noted that he had a terrific employer and for that he was extremely grateful. His employer, to whom he feels a great loyalty, was genuinely concerned for the wellbeing of their 3000-plus staff. Gratitude helped him feel fortunate and recognise the good in the world around him. It helped him to accept and stop pining for a lost past.

Purpose: He reminded himself that part of his role and responsibility was to look after the many hundreds of staff that reported to him. This alone gave him a reason to start work in the morning, even if it was only walking to the kitchen bench. Working for state government, part of his role was to actively manage Victorians though Covid and into the future. This strongly aligned with his purpose of helping others. He also took the time to reconsider where he was best placed to fulfil those dreams and desires both at work and outside of it.

Routine: After working with me and accepting that things may be like this for a long time, he designed and has stuck to a 'working from home' routine that now sees him have quality time 'off' and quality time 'on'. He also set himself up a legitimate and functional working space in the spare room, where he is less likely to be interrupted by daily life in the kitchen.

Self-Awareness: With his whole world turned upside-down, he needed to monitor his moods, feelings, emotions and needs. His Self-Awareness Anchor was vital for him to determine the best way to care for himself, his family and his staff.

Health: Attention to diet, sleep and exercise enabled him to be the person he needed to be to help others. He became acutely aware of building a solid, healthy self-care component into each and every day. Never allowing himself, as I regularly reminded him, to get 'too tired, too hungry, or too thirsty'.

Resilience: Curiously, he didn't mention Resilience in his talk to the group. Even though he was practising it, he didn't recognise it at the time.

He and I spoke about the significant challenges he was facing. Many of his staff were stuck in the Difficulty Phase, which made their work and lives challenging. Many were trying their best but were looking back, hoping for 'normal' to return and feeling exhausted and disconnected. As a senior executive in his organisation, he realised his role was to help shift people through to the Acceptance Phase. He also realised that attending to any one of the Anchors would help his staff shift slightly further away from the Difficulty Phase and build their resilience.

> ### ✎ Resilience in Action
> If you work, answer the following questions about your workplace stress in your Learning Journal:
> - Thinking about your work specifically, on a scale of 1–10 how stressful is it?
> - What is it that causes your stress at work?
> - What can you control?
> - What can you do to manage better through workplace stress?
> - Pick one or two to start doing now.

What the research says

In his 2002 book, *Aging Well*, Harvard University psychologist George Vaillant describes resilient individuals as resembling 'a twig with a fresh, green living core. When twisted out of shape, such a twig bends, but it does not break; instead it springs back and continues growing.' Dean Becker, the president and CEO of Adaptiv Learning Systems, has said, 'More than education, more than experience, more than training, a person's level of resilience will determine who succeeds and who fails. That's true in the cancer ward, it's true in the Olympics, and it's true in the boardroom' (Coutu, 2002).

When I first learned of the expression 'We live in a VUCA world', I didn't really get it, at least until Covid struck. VUCA stands for volatile, uncertain, complex and ambiguous. Incidents caused by weather disasters, geopolitics, pandemic outbreaks, scientific and technological innovation and other non-human control factors happen frequently. Even the strongest among us are significantly challenged. But I am interested in why some people suffer real hardships and others manage well. It's a question that's fascinated me ever since my mother was struck down with her debilitating and, at the time, incurable illness. Witnessing her 'never give up' attitude, despite having a disease-riddled body, and beating the odds repeatedly, had an impact. Incredibly, she overcame tremendous hardship and outlived her disease. She epitomised cognitive hardiness and was extraordinarily resilient.

She assessed her needs and dealt with hardships. Resilient individuals have seven traits, according to the National Alliance on Mental Illness (Vahidi, 2021). These people are flexible, are willing to learn, they seek solutions and they are resourceful. They are also creative and set realistic expectations. In my research and through client experience I have seen repeatedly that this ability of understanding the current situation and manage through, differentiates the best from the rest. Whether or not you have it depends largely on how your life unfolds and you only find out when you're faced with obstacles, stress or environmental threats. Resilience can also change over time, but the good news is that you can learn to be resilient.

Resilience Toolkit

Topics covered:
- building blocks
- resilience at work
- a closer look at crisis
- the impact of attitudes
- growth mindset
- preventing burnout.

Building blocks

There is no single accepted set of building blocks for resilience, but there is agreement on some of the contributing factors: wellness, connection, healthy perception, which includes self-compassion, optimism, humour and meaning. Focusing on these elements can empower us to withstand and learn from our difficulties and challenges.

Perception counts. How we think about the world plays a very big role in our ability to cope. According to George Bonanno, a clinical psychologist who specialises in resilience, we can make ourselves more or less vulnerable by how we think about things. When we have a healthy optimistic view of reality it helps us stay positive about what lies ahead, even when faced with seemingly insurmountable obstacles. There's a beautiful quote by Victor Frankl, in his book *Man's Search for Meaning*, that captures this idea, 'Everything can be taken from a man but one thing: the last of the human freedoms – to choose one's attitude in any given set of circumstances, to choose one's own way.'

Equally, when we can make meaning of terrible times and feel we have a specific purpose in life we are more likely to recover from failure or disappointment. The 'How can this be happening to me?' response places people as victims, which carries no lessons for them. Resilient people devise constructs about their suffering to create some sort of meaning for themselves and others. When my daughter was gravely unwell, I would remind myself of who I am as a person and who I needed to be so that I could help her survive her challenges. I saw it as no coincidence that I had many of the skills needed to care for her quite simply because of my profession. My professional and home life were blending. The dynamic of making meaning is, most researchers agree, the way resilient people build bridges from present-day hardships to a fuller, better constructed future.

Having a healthy sense of humour and being able to laugh at your own misfortune puts you at an advantage when it comes to bouncing back. As is having a strong and clear moral compass with a set of beliefs about right and wrong. When you are willing to leave your comfort zone and confront your fears you are more likely to overcome your challenges and grow as a person. I learned to advocate for my daughter and regularly challenged very senior players in the medical fraternity when I didn't agree with their decisions. From this, she received a better quality of care and ultimately better health outcomes.

A big part of individual resilience is being able to treat and care for yourself with empathy and compassion – in *both* the good and the bad times. Take it from me, it is no easy task stepping aside to take time out for yourself in the midst of what may appear to be a crisis. It can be as simple as stepping outside to get some fresh air when you've been sitting in a small hospital room since the early morning. All too often I've seen people put everybody else first only to burn out and pay a high price for neglecting themselves. Listening and responding to our own needs ultimately allows us to have better clarity of thought.

People who have a strong social support network and positive relationships are better equipped to bounce back from loss or disappointment. This is also why the Relationships Anchor is so important. Resilient individuals try to engage others rather than alienate them. They see problems as opportunities to strengthen relationships. They feel secure with people they trust. Connecting with empathy and understanding people reminds you that you're not alone in the midst of difficulties. Additionally, those who have a role model in mind can draw strength from their desire to emulate this person. I do not know how I would have managed through all the outrageous and seemingly insurmountable difficulties I had to face with my daughter had I not had such an incredible inner circle of support and love around me.

Resilience at work

Everybody will at some point receive criticism or experience a failure at work and it tests our resilience. Increased responsibility, forward progress, and significant positive events all result in the need for adaptation and recovery (Youssef & Luthans, 2007). You might have a fear of presenting in front of an audience, feel frustrated after receiving negative feedback, or guilty about not spending enough time with your family, and all of these can affect your professional and personal development if you don't face them. So, how do you know if your resilience is waning? Your emotions let you know (Reivich and Shatté, 2002). When you react with these emotions disproportionately or repeatedly to an event that occurred, your resilience may not be robust enough:

- anger
- sadness or depression
- guilt
- anxiety or fear
- embarrassment

A closer look at crisis

A few weeks into Covid, I started to notice that people around me were responding differently to lockdown. Covid seemed to magnify both our strengths and our weaknesses. Some flourished while others really struggled. There were three distinct groups:

1. Some panicked and were frightened, unsure of what to do, how to behave or where to go.
2. Some remained calm and followed commonsense advice, as it came through.
3. Some resisted change and tried desperately to hang on to the idea that before long things would go 'back to normal'.

Each group acted differently. Some saw the lockdown environment as suffocating and threatening and were waiting for the 'all clear'. Others held it flexibly, and rather than feeling constrained, saw it as an opportunity to revamp and reconnect. More significantly, these people examined their life and found new ways to do things. I found ways to deliver my programs online and work with clients seamlessly, from the comfort of my own home. I also loved the fact that I could spend more time with the kids. As a rule we ate lunch together and took mini walking breaks in the garden or out with the dogs to help break up the monotony of being in the one place.

The impact of attitudes

There are many factors that influence who we are and how we do what we do: mindset is one of them. Your mindset is a set of beliefs, assumptions and attitudes, some of which are likely well below the surface sitting in the non-conscious part of your brain. Research findings from Tel Aviv University will come as no surprise that our attitude towards stress greatly impacts our subsequent approach to handling it (Ben-Avi et al., 2018). They use the term 'stress mindset' to help explain the alternative way to approach life's challenges. It is a mindset where individuals believe that stress has enhancing versus debilitating consequences. Think about it. Do you think you have the same attitude toward a particular debilitating stress as your partner? If so, you would then expect them to be as unhappy as you under the same stress level. Their findings suggest that, if you and your partner have a stress-mindset mismatch, you'll be less understanding toward your partner.

Dealing with change or loss is an inevitable part of our lives. How we deal with these problems can play a significant role in the outcome and the long-term psychological consequences. Resilient people use their skills and strengths to recover from problems and challenges. They face life's difficulties head on. They still experience grief or anxiety, yet they handle it in ways that foster strength and growth. The symbol for resilience in Japanese Kanji also means elasticity, flexibility and adaptability, with the power to recover, restore and rehabilitate. As I write this now, it's 3 pm and I've just tucked my daughter up in bed. She's been crying and she's feeling dreadful and flat. Life is still a struggle for her these days. It's times like these that she needs love and acceptance. It's not a time for lectures or accusations. Her 'time out' will give her the chance to rest, slow down, and when she's ready, she will shift her perspective. These tough times for her will pass. They always do. She knows it. I know it. She's not giving in. She's caring for herself.

There are three main attitudes and beliefs that have a significant impact on our resilience (Sheldon & Lyubomirsky, 2006). The first is the amount of belief you have in your own ability to succeed and accomplish the things you set out to. It's also about how much influence (control) you feel you have over the big things in your life. In other words, do you feel responsible for where you are in your life or was it just luck? The second is how you feel about challenges and change and whether you think they are empowering opportunities. It's around how determined and committed, or not, you are to make those challenges a success, despite the struggles. Lastly, resilient people have self-confidence, a positive belief in themselves and their overall personal value. This has the added benefit of leading to a positive mood (Sheldon, 2006). Low self-worth, on the other hand, with constant self-criticism can lead to feeling sad, angry, depressed, anxious, shame or guilt.

Resilience in Action

Answer the following questions in your Learning Journal:

Thinking about your attitudes and beliefs specifically, on a scale of 1–10 respond to the following questions, where 10 is true all the time and 1 is never true:

1. I view life's changes as opportunities, empowering and challenging.
2. I believe I have influence (control) over the significant outcomes in my life.
3. I have many positive feelings and thoughts about my self-worth and my personal value.

Consider where your strengths and development opportunities are to build your personal resilience.

Growth mindset

A pessimist sees the difficulty in every opportunity;
an optimist sees the opportunity in every difficulty.
—Winston Churchill

One of the most basic beliefs we carry about ourselves has to do with how we view and inhabit what we consider to be our personality. Carol Dweck famously categorised these views into two mindsets (2006). You either have a fixed or a growth mindset. Those with a fixed mindset think they can't change in any meaningful way. They're stuck with their character, intelligence and creative ability. They believe they have what they were born with. Alternatively, those with a growth mindset love challenges and see failure as an opportunity for stretching their existing abilities. From a very early age these two mindsets determine a great deal of our behaviour. If you believe your talents can be developed through hard work, good strategies, and input from others, you have a growth mindset.

There is also some emerging positive research suggesting that mindset may hold the solution to fighting stress. Seeing the world through the lens of growth enables you to shift your thoughts away from the negative focus induced by stress and back toward the positive. From personal experience, I have no doubt that this is true. The counselling work I have done with clients, helping them reconsider their attitudes has helped them overcome incredible difficulties. When we learn to accept our feelings, and make room for them, rather than fight them, all sorts of possibilities open up. To cultivate a growth mindset ask yourself: 'What can I learn from the situation to better develop my skills?' Find a way to embrace challenges and keep going when facing setbacks. Embrace effort and difficulty as a pathway to being better. Be open to criticism and learn from it. Find lessons and be inspired by the success of others. Finally, be aware of your mindset and how you speak to yourself and others.

Here are some growth areas you might like to think about:

- Is there **something you've always wanted to do** but were afraid you wouldn't be good at? Well, now's the time. Make a plan. Look for opportunities for learning and growth for yourself and other people. Identify why you want to grow and make learning goals a regular part of your plans. The rationale will keep you in there, even when you feel like you are not making any progress. Be playful and flexible in your learning. Not everyone learns the same way. If one way doesn't work, be willing to try another, and another, until you find one that suits your learning style.
- **Do you give up too easily?** Next time you are enjoying something, but finding it hard to make progress, put yourself in a growth mindset. There's a performance dip early in the learning curve: if you push through it your learning will improve. Do you feel discouraged when a project runs into obstacles, throwing it off your original timeline? Think about the extra effort you need to put into the project as a constructive force, not a big drag.
- **When others outperform you**, do you just assume they are smarter or more talented? It's more likely that they used better strategies, taught themselves more, practised harder, and worked their way through obstacles. Find ways to learn about the efforts of high performers. How do you use praise? Find time to celebrate your own growth, learning and processes. Reward and celebrate the behaviour you want in yourself and in others.
- What kind of people do you invite into your **circle of friends**? Who do you bring onto your work team? Surround yourself with people who aren't afraid to provide constructive criticism. Do you feel judged or bitter when

someone criticises your decisions or actions? See if you can view these occasions as an opportunity to better understand the outcomes and impact of your decisions. Front up to your imperfections, acknowledge them and find ways to accept them.
- **Do you admire someone** who seems to achieve great things with little effort? Find out about their journey. Learn about the great effort and mistakes that went into their accomplishments.
- Start adopting **open language** such as 'yet' or 'trying to learn how to', rather than 'can't', 'never', and 'always'. If you think you are no good at sharing your ideas with others, it gives you permission to be bad at it, or worse, not speak up. Try thinking, 'I am working on being better at sharing my ideas with others.'

✎ Resilience in Action

Choose an area or a challenge that you are currently facing and would like to improve, record it in your Learning Journal.

Below are some suggestions to get you thinking:
- something you've always wanted to do
- something you keep giving up but want to stick to
- a person who outperforms you, and you would like to exceed their achievements
- someone you admire and want to emulate.

Pick out one or two of the above suggestions that you are willing to incorporate into your daily routine to meet that challenge area. Capture why this challenge is important for you.

Share your challenge with someone else who can help hold you accountable.

Preventing burnout

Burnout is a state of emotional, physical and mental exhaustion which leaves you feeling at rock bottom, alone and unable to cope. You struggle to function and, sadly, it's not something a couple of nights' sleep can fix. It happens to the very best of us and it doesn't happen overnight. Preventing burnout is about managing yourself well with the reality of the workload and stresses you are facing. Recognising the signs and getting help early is important for recovering quickly. If you feel really out of control, you need to tap into your resources and ask for help. Friends, colleagues, family, your doctor are all possible options. It's something that I had to learn to do. As an independent, high-functioning businesswoman and mum, it was not easy for me to ask for help. But doing so, allowed me to share the load and even switch off at times so that I could find precious time to recover from the stresses of managing my daughter's condition. Below are four easy-to-access ideas to help shield you from burnout.

The first is to use good old Vitamin C (ascorbic acid) to help your body's stress response system. Your adrenal glands need Vitamin C to stay healthy and manufacture the adrenal hormones that cope with stress, particularly cortisol. When we are stressed our bodies use up Vitamin C. So whether you're exercising in an aerobics class (good stress) or dealing with a heavy life situation (bad stress), you'll benefit from vitamin C. Without it, your whole body can feel ongoing fatigue (even with rest), have a weakened immune response, decreased joy, increased frustration, and inability to handle even the smallest of stresses. And no one wants that. The more cortisol you make, the more vitamin C you use. Ensuring you have a healthy diet with fresh fruit and veggies is the best way to get it.

Second, slowing down how you start your day helps lower the cortisol in your system from that initial spike that got you out of bed. You can remedy this with a quick meditation or some mindful breathing to pace yourself and ease into the day, helping you feel calmer and more able to cope with the stresses of the day.

Third, scheduling time for breaks and reducing stimulus allows your cortisol levels to settle in your body. Look for opportunities to take several small time-outs during the day. Even a five-minute break every hour is beneficial and better than one 30-minute break in a six-hour block. It's common sense, but when we are up against it, trying to push work out and keep productivity high, having breaks seems counter-intuitive. Research fully supports the long-term benefits on productivity of having regular short breaks, including that so-often-missed lunch break. Big breaks are also important. Holidays give us something to look forward to and boost our system with great memories and lovely feel-good endorphins.

One of my favourite tips is spending time outside – in the garden, a park or in nature. I call this green time. The Japanese call it Forest Bathing. Early research shows that Forest Bathing may boost your immune system, reduce blood pressure, lower cortisol levels, improve concentration and memory. Other research reported that walking in a forest for 15 minutes saw people with less anxiety, hostility, fatigue, confusion, and depressive symptoms, and more vigour (Song, et al., 2018). Think about the last time you took a walk in the forest and how good you felt afterwards. Ah, even writing about green time makes me feel good!

The final tip sits with your digital technology. To make it work for you, you need to actively figure out what your devices do for you.

I want my phone to:

- Help me communicate meaningfully with people I care about.
- Look up the answers to questions when I have them.
- Help me navigate.
- Monitor my to-do list and calendar and personal notes.
- Entertain me, but in a way that lifts me up and isn't merely burning time.

I don't want my phone to:

- Interrupt whatever it is I'm doing unless it's really urgent.
- Eat up time without a purpose or convince me to do not-important-and-not-urgent things.
- Convince me to buy things I don't really need.
- Bring down my happiness.
- Interrupt my sleep patterns.

> **✎ Resilience in Action**
>
> To manage your stress and help mitigate burnout, capture in your Learning Journal how you can:
>
> - Incorporate more Vitamin C into your diet.
> - Slow yourself down in your morning routine.
> - Incorporate green time regularly throughout your day.
> - Consider your phone use.
>
> What are five things that your smartphone does that cost you money, focus, time and positivity without giving you much in return?
>
> - List four to five things you want your phone to do.
> - List four to five things you don't you want your phone to do.

Anchor Self – Resilience

Take some time out to conduct your Resilience DIY Assessment.

Give yourself a score out of 10, where 10 is true all of the time and 1 is never true.

Resilience	1–10
I persevere in tough times	
I call on my relationships for support when facing difficulties	
I have full influence (control) over the significant outcomes in my life	
I maintain a growth mindset at all times	
I ensure I have a degree of challenge to enhance my life	
I never doubt my self-worth	
I always adopt a flexible attitude to change and challenges	
I actively incorporate activities to build my resilience	
Resilience TOTAL	

When you have added up your score, out of a total of 80, colour in your Resilience Anchor score on the circumplex. Use the Scoring Key as your guide.[*]

---

[*] At the end of the book, your individual Anchor scores can be translated across to form your Anchor Self-profile.

RESILIENCE

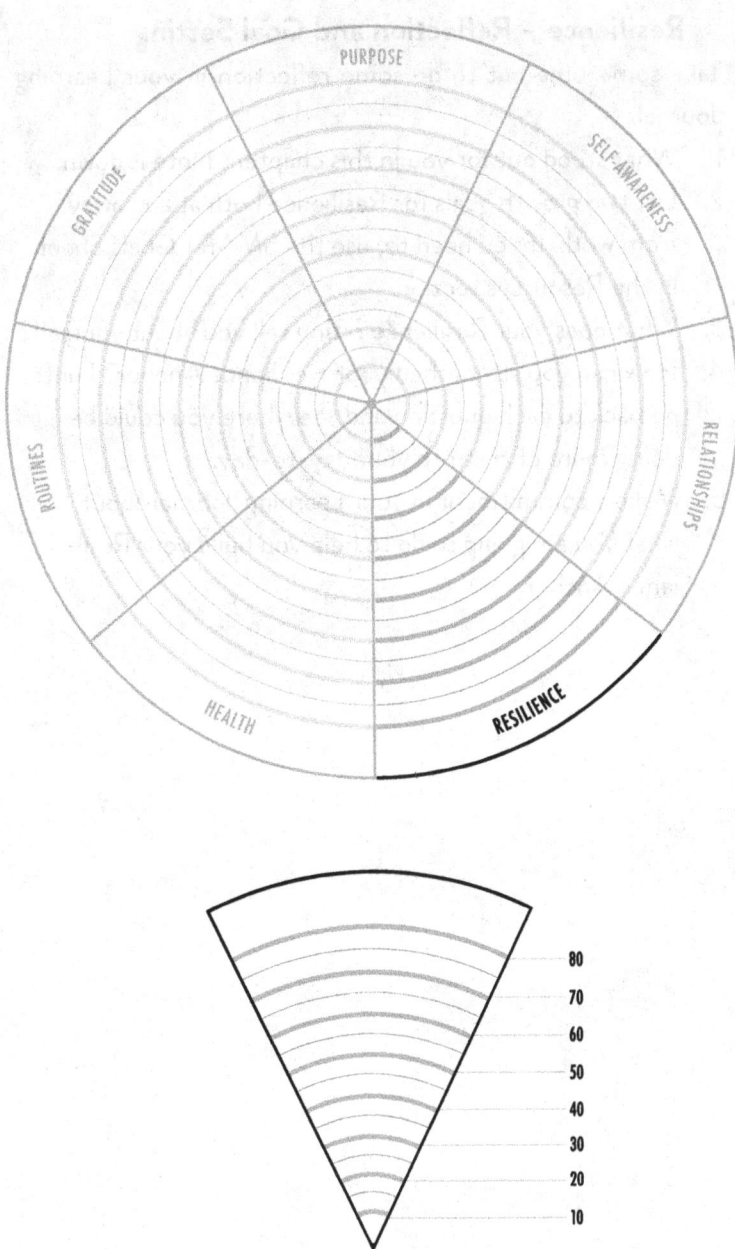

Scoring Key

✎ Resilience – Reflection and Goal Setting

Take some time out to do some reflection in your Learning Journal.

1. What stood out for you in this chapter? Note it down.
2. List two growth goals for Resilience both at and away from work. If you need to, use the SMART Goals Sheet in the Resources section.
3. What does your Resilience rating tell you about yourself?
4. How can you strengthen your Resilience Anchor? Hint: go back to each question and see where you could be doing more of this into your day-to-day.
5. Make a commitment in your Learning Journal about what you are going to do to help you build your Resilience Anchor.

12

Your Anchor Self

Now that you've worked your way through all 7 Anchors, you can do the 7 Anchors Inventory™ Self-Description.

✎ Instructions: For each of the following statements give yourself a score out of 10, where 10 is true all of the time and 1 is never true. Add up your score for each Anchor, out of a total of 80. If you have done the exercise at the end of each Anchor, just copy your values over. Mark your score on the circumplex to create Your Anchor Self, using the scoring key as your guide. The central ring is 10, the next ring is 20, all the way through to the outer ring, which is 80.

Self-Awareness	**1–10**
I have an excellent understanding of my strengths	
I have a clear sense of how I am feeling throughout the day	
I have an excellent understanding of my weaknesses	
I know when one of my 'hot buttons' is being pressed	
I manage myself well at all times	
I have a clear understanding of my values	
I know why I think and behave the way I do	
I welcome feedback from others	
Self-Awareness TOTAL	

Purpose	1–10
I understand my purpose in life	
In my day to day, I know what gives meaning to my life	
My decisions about what I do are always worthwhile	
People who I work closely with know my life's purpose	
I feel motivated to make the most of every day	
I make decisions so that I do not live with regret	
I have the courage to live out my life's purpose	
I have values and beliefs that help me know who I am	
Purpose TOTAL	

Relationships	1–10
I like who I am	
I support and encourage myself	
My self-talk is positive and encouraging	
I have trusted work relationships	
I have a solid group of friends whom I am close to	
There are a few work colleagues with whom I can truly be myself	
When I am going through difficulty, I always have one or two people who know	
I can have difficult conversations without negative repercussions	
Relationships TOTAL	

Gratitude	1–10
I have a very long list of things to be grateful for	
When I'm going through difficulties, I always think of the good things that I have	
I am always grateful for the gifts and talents I have	
I always offer thanks and/or prayers for what I have received	
Being grateful helps me navigate through difficulties	
I am grateful for the opportunity to contribute to finding better solutions	
I highly value the friendship and love I get from people close to me	
I always acknowledge my appreciation to others at work	
Gratitude TOTAL	

Health	1–10
I have a good understanding of my health	
Overall, I am physically fit and well	
I take good care of my physical health daily	
I always make healthy food choices	
I always get a good night's sleep (7–9 hours)	
When I feel flat, I look after myself well	
I use wellbeing strategies to keep my mind healthy	
I have balance in my day	
Health TOTAL	

Routines	1–10
I get the most out of each day	
My day is planned	
I have balance in my day	
I am aware of the habits that don't serve me well	
I always focus on being more efficient	
I have clear boundaries between work and outside work	
I am always doing what I am meant to be doing	
I judge accurately how long something will take to do	
Routines TOTAL	

Resilience	1–10
I persevere in tough times	
I call on my relationships for support when facing difficulties	
I have full influence (control) over the significant outcomes in my life	
I maintain a growth mindset at all times	
I ensure I have a degree of challenge to enhance my life	
I never doubt my self-worth	
I always adopt a flexible attitude to change and challenges	
I actively incorporate activities to build my resilience	
Resilience TOTAL	

YOUR ANCHOR SELF

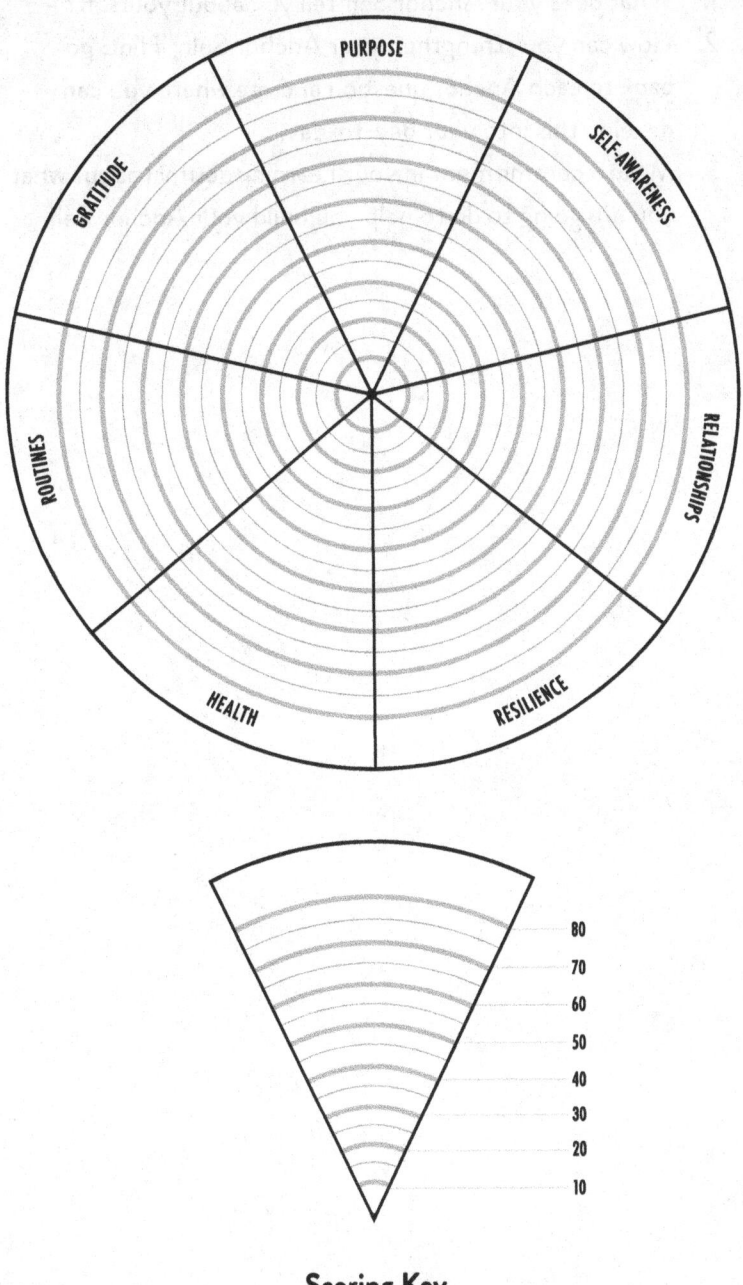

Scoring Key

Your Anchor Self
1. What does your Anchor Self tell you about yourself?
2. How can you strengthen your Anchor Self? Hint: go back to each Anchor question and see where you can develop this into your day-to-day.
3. Make a commitment in your Learning Journal about what you are going to do to help you build your Anchor Self.

Conclusion

Dear Reader, the 7 Anchors helped me write this book. There were times when I had so much going on that I was stretched to the max. I was still running my busy practice, looking after my daughter who was in and out of care, the family, all our pets, the house and all the other things that I like to do in my life. I wanted to write a book, but I knew all of the other priorities also needed managing. It was my Purpose that kept me motivated – I want to help others. I'm blessed to be able to spend my working days sharing the 7 Anchors with leaders and teams throughout Australia. I want to help people who don't have easy access to this information, people who might not have the means to access coaching and counselling.

To write this book I engaged a friend of mine (aka my writing coach) to hold me accountable to a writing schedule. The process was emergent as I'd never written a book before and didn't have the faintest idea how to go about it. We met regularly (over Zoom) and agreed timelines along the way. At each meeting we would discuss the work I'd submitted. In the beginning writing felt a bit weird, even though I was full of enthusiasm and energy. But there were days and times when other parts of my life took over and it was a struggle. On these days when we happened to meet, my coach just gently stepped me back to the 7 Anchors and asked me which Anchor I needed to help me get back on track. As you can see, it worked!

If you thought you couldn't do something that's important to you before reading this book, I hope by now you're actively engaging with the 7 Anchors to prove to yourself that you can. Difficulties and challenges are a part of life. They've been a very big part of my life for the last four years, some of which I have shared with you in these pages. And, without exception, all of my clients also face difficult times. The whole world faced a volatile and uncertain difficulty when it came up against Covid-19. We need to live with and through difficulties and not be bound by them at the exclusion of all the other parts of our lives.

During Covid-19 I saw some people thrive and others flounder. Those that managed well used levers that I've seen high performers use for decades. Writing this book through that period made me even more aware of the relationship between discipline and a great life. To live a great life, we need to be disciplined enough to park our feelings in the passenger seat. We need to learn to keep doing things regardless of how we are feeling. We need to set up Routines that touch on all of our Anchors, to offer ourselves certainty that the world will not hand to us.

The 7 Anchor model provides a methodology to face life, to be your best and to thrive, with more confidence and ease. When you consciously use the 7 Anchors to guide your decisions and behaviours, you will navigate through at your best, and have the added bonus of enjoying your life along the way.

None of this is easy. It takes commitment, discipline, patience, kindness, work and self-compassion. I only heard about some research today that found self-compassion is a greater predictor of success than self-confidence. Be kind to yourself when you inevitably 'slip up' or stray off track. Ask yourself which Anchor you need most at the moment, open up this book and read the Anchor – even if you've already read it ten times. I guarantee you that a different level of understanding will emerge each time. The 7 Anchors will help you weather the storms and guide you back on track to accomplish more than you ever thought possible.

Please feel free to get in touch if you'd like to share your story and how the 7 Anchors have helped you or your team: trina@7anchors.au

SMART Goal Template

SMART Goals are designed to help you identify if what you want to achieve is realistic and to determine a deadline for it. When writing SMART Goals use concise language and include relevant information. These are designed to help you succeed, so be positive when answering the questions.

Initial Goal (Write the goal you have in mind):
_____
_____
_____
_____
_____

1. Specific (What do you want to accomplish? Who needs to be included? When do you want to do this? Why is this a goal?):
_____
_____
_____
_____
_____

2. Measurable (How can you measure progress and know if you've successfully met your goal?):

_____
_____
_____
_____
_____
_____

3. Achievable (Do you have the skills required to achieve the goal? If not, can you obtain them? What is the motivation for this goal? Is the amount of effort required on par with what the goal will achieve?):

_____
_____
_____
_____
_____
_____
_____

4. Relevant (Why am I setting this goal now? Does it align with who I want and need to be?):

_____
_____
_____
_____
_____
_____

SMART GOAL TEMPLATE

5. Time-bound (What's the deadline and is it realistic?):
_____
_____
_____
_____
_____
_____
_____
_____

SMART Goal (Review what you have written, and craft a new goal statement based on what the answers to the questions above have revealed):
_____
_____
_____
_____
_____
_____
_____
_____
_____

Milestone(s) and Deadline(s):
_____
_____
_____
_____
_____
_____
_____
_____

Acknowledgements

Many people have been involved directly or indirectly in the writing of this book. To those who physically helped me by reading, brainstorming and editing. To Carole Lydon, Julia Bourne, Paul Saunders, Janet Munro, Jen Saul, Ken Whitters, Chrisafina Rick, Robyn Cottew, Arne Rubinstein and Catriona Wallace. I am happy to be able to call all of you friends. To Dieter Weinand, who coached me patiently through the writing and eventual publishing of this book. To Peter Hayward, who has mentored me for many years and continues to support and inspire me to stay on my path. You have given me so much knowledge in the form of countless books, podcasts and thought-provoking conversations over fabulous lunches on the nature of people and the choices they make in life and career. Your generosity of spirit is astonishing and I can truly say that none of this work would have happened if you had not been there to encourage me from the beginning, through the entire journey to publication!

To the incredible people I have worked with in the last twenty years, as clients, all over Australia. Together we have been through some sh!t. I have witnessed how you have positively impacted the lives of many hundreds of people. There are too many of you to name but I know that as a result of your continuing work in leadership of self and others, in your work and in your life, the positive ripple effects to help others navigate through their challenges are, and will continue to be, far reaching. I have been so privileged to work with you, some for many years,

ACKNOWLEDGEMENTS

in different roles in your work and life and bear witness to the amazing transformations you go through. To my phenomenal colleagues who continue to inspire me in the work that you do – again, too many of you to name, but you know who you are! Thank you for your encouragement and unwavering faith that this book would happen.

To Dave Pitcher, for helping me raise our two wonderful kids to be such incredible young adults. And gosh, we have had our challenges along the way! I am very grateful for the wonderful father you are.

Finally, to Penny and Archie. You were the inspiration for this book. You have taught me so much about why I get out of bed in the morning and to face the day with courage, patience and compassion. I am so proud to have you both in my life. You are the most amazing kids a mother could ever wish for. And for that I thank you both. You have taught me about what is important in life. Your courage, strength, wisdom, gifts and talents leave me in awe. I love who we are and what we have together. I look forward to many more adventures, fun and laughter. I am excited for your future and for the contributions you will make. I love each of you to the moon and back, even though you still drive me a bit crazy at times.

Bibliography

PART ONE

Australian Bureau of Statistics (Life Expectancy, 2017–2019, 2020) *Life tables, Statistics about life tables for Australia, states and territories and life expectancy at birth estimates for sub-state regions* https://www.abs.gov.au/statistics/people/population/life-tables/latest-release.

Baughman, D. Healthy Communicating. (2013). *Liberating Assumptions.* https://www.healthycommunicating.com/s/Chapter-1-Liberating-Assumptions.pdf

Berinato, S. (2020). That Discomfort You're Feeling is Grief, *Harvard Business Review*, 23 March https://hbr.org/2020/03/thatdiscomfort-youre-feeling-is-grief.

Clear, J. (2021). *3-2-1: On allowing yourself to be happy and full, and how small errors compound* https://jamesclear.com/3-2-1/march-11-2021.

Covey, S. R. (2004). *The 7 habits of highly effective people: Restoring the character ethic* ([Rev. ed.].). Free Press.

Gardner, H. (1983). *Frames of mind: The theory of multiple intelligences.* New York: Basic Books.

Gardner, H. (2000). *Intelligence reframed: Multiple intelligences for the 21st century.* Hachette UK.

Gawande, A. (2014). *Being mortal: Medicine and what matters in the end.* Metropolitan Books/Henry Holt and Company.

Goleman, D., Boyatzis, R. (2017). Emotional Intelligence Has 12 Elements. Which Do You Need to Work On? *Harvard Business Review*, 6 Feb.

Jordan, S. (2013). *The Oracle & Omaha: How Warren Buffett and His Hometown Shaped Each Other*. Omaha WORLD-Herald.

Kübler-Ross, E., & Kessler, D. (2005). *On grief and grieving: Finding the meaning of grief through the five stages of loss*. New York: Scribner.

Palmer, B., Donaldson, C., Stough C., (2002). Emotional intelligence and life satisfaction. *Personality and Individual Differences*, 33(7), 1091–1100.

Pestle, Jonathan L. (2009). Oxford Dictionary of Business and Management (5th ed.)

Plomin, R., Fulker D.W., Corley, R., DeFries, J.C. (1997). Nature, Nurture, and Cognitive Development from 1 to 16 Years: A Parent-Offspring Adoption Study. *Psychological Science*, 8(6), 442–447.

Sinek, S. (2011). *Start with why: How great leaders inspire everyone to take action*. Harlow, England: Penguin Books.

Sternberg, Robert. (2003). A Broad View of Intelligence: The Theory of Successful Intelligence. *Consulting Psychology Journal: Practice and Research*, 55(3), 139–154.

PART TWO

Anchor 1 – Self-Awareness

Brown, B. (2010). *The gifts of imperfection: let go of who you think you're supposed to be and embrace who you are*. Center City, Minnesota, Hazelden Publishing. pp. 20.

Bryant, F.B., & Veroff, J. (2007). *Savoring: A new model of positive experience*. Mahwah, NJ: Lawrence Erlbaum Associates.

Capobianco, S., Davis, M., & Kraus, L. (1999). *Managing conflict dynamics: A practical approach*. St. Petersburg, FL: Eckerd College Leadership Development Institute.

Casali, N., Feraco, T., Ghisi, M., & Meneghetti, C. (2020). "Andrà tutto bene": Associations between character strengths, psychological distress and self-efficacy during COVID-19 lockdown. *Journal of Happiness Studies*, 22(5), 2255–2274. doi.org/10.1007/s10902-020-00321-w.

Drucker, P.F. (1967). *The Effective Executive*. Harper & Row Publishers, New York.

Drucker, P.F. (2008). *Managing Oneself.* USA: Harvard Business School.

Drummond, T. (2021). Vocabulary of emotions [PDF]. https://tomdrummond.com/leading-and-caring-for-children/emotion-vocabulary/).

Ekman, P. (1992). Facial Expressions of Emotion: New Findings, New Questions. *Psychological Science.* 3 (1): 34-38. doi:10.1111/j.1467-9280.1992.tb00253.

Eurich, T. (2018). What self-awareness really is (and how to cultivate it). Retrieved from https://hbr.org/2018/01/what-self-awareness really is and how to cultivate it.

Evans, P., Hargreaves, D.J. & Conde, J. (2010). *Values-driven leadership.* Prahran, Vic: Tilde University Press.

Flade, P., Asplund, J., & Elliot, G. (2015). Employees who use their strengths outperform those who don't. 8 Oct. https://www.gallup.com/workplace/236561/employees-strengths-outperform-don.aspx.

Goleman, D. (2007). *Emotional Intelligence* (10th ed.). Bantam Books.

Gong, Z., Chen, Y., & Wang, Y. (2019). The Influence of Emotional Intelligence on Job Burnout and Job Performance: Mediating Effect of Psychological Capital. *Frontiers in psychology,* 10, 2707. doi.org/10.3389/fpsyg.2019.02707.

Harter, J., Schmidt, F., Agrawal, S., Blue, A., Plowman, S., Josh, P., & Asplund, J. (2020).The Relationship Between Engagement at Work and Organizational Outcomes 2020 Q12® Meta-Analysis: 10th Ed.

Law, K., Wong, C., Huang, E., & Li, X. (2008). The effects of emotional intelligence on job performance and life satisfaction for the research and development scientists in China. *Asia Pacific Journal of Management,* 25(1), 51–69. doi.org/10.1007/s10490-007-9062-3.

Mayer, G.J., Finn, S.E., Eyde, L.D., Kay, G.G., Moreland, K.L., Dies, R.R., Eisman, E.J., Kubiszyn, T.W. and Reed, G.M. (2001). Psychological testing and psychological assessment: a review of evidence and issues. *American Psychologist,* 56(2), 128–65.

Mayer, J.D. and Salovey, P. (1997). What is emotional intelligence?, In Salovey, P. and Sluyter, D.J. (Eds.), *Emotional Development and Emotional Intelligence: Implications for Educators,* pp. 3–34. Basic Books, New York, NY.

Miao, C., Humphrey, R.H. and Qian, S. (2018). Emotional intelligence and authentic leadership: a meta-analysis, *Leadership & Organization Development Journal*, 39(5), 679–690. doi.org/10.1108/LODJ-02-2018-0066.

Niemiec, Ryan M. (2019). Six functions of character strengths for thriving at times of adversity and opportunity: a theoretical perspective. *Applied Research in Quality of Life*. doi.org/10.1007/s11482-018-9692-2.

O'Boyle, E.H., Humphrey, R.H., Pollack, J.M., Hawver, T.H., & Story, P.A. (2011). The relation between emotional intelligence and job performance: A meta-analysis. *Journal of Organizational Behavior*, 32, 788–818.

Palmer, B., Donaldson, C. and Stough, C. (2002). Emotional intelligence and life satisfaction, *Personality and Individual Differences*, 33(7), 1091–1100, ISSN 0191-8869, doi.org/10.1016/S0191-8869(01)00215-X. (https://www.sciencedirect.com/science/article/pii/S019188690100215X).

Park, J., Wood, J., Bondi, C., Del Arco, A., Moghaddam, B. (2016). Anxiety Evokes Hypofrontality and Disrupts Rule-Relevant Encoding by Dorsomedial Prefrontal Cortex Neurons. *Journal of Neuroscience*, 36 (11) 3322–3335. doi: 10.1523/jneurosci.4250-15.2016.

Paul E. Jose, Bee T. Lim & Fred B. Bryant (2012) Does savoring increase happiness? A daily diary study, *The Journal of Positive Psychology*, 7:3, 176–187, DOI: 10.1080/17439760.2012.671345.

Schwarzer, R., & Jerusalem, M. (1995). Generalized Self-Efficacy scale. In J. Weinman, S. Wright, & M. Johnston, Measures in health psychology: A user›s portfolio. Causal and control beliefs (pp. 35–37). Windsor, UK: NFER-NELSON.

Tuckman, B.W. and Sexton, T.L. (1990). The relation between self-beliefs and self-regulated performance. *Journal of Social Behavior and Personality*, 5, 465–472.

Turow, S. (2005). *Ordinary Heroes*. Farrar, Straus and Giroux, NY.

Wen, J., Huang, S.S., and Hou, P. (2019). Emotional intelligence, emotional labor, perceived organizational support, and job satisfaction: a moderated mediation model. *International Journal of Healthcare Management*. 81, 120–130. doi: 10.1016/j.ijhm.2019.01.009.

Wilson, K.G. & Groom, J. (2002). *The Valued Living Questionnaire*. Available from Kelly Wilson.

Zenger, J.H., Folkman, J.R., Edinger, S.K. (2011) Making yourself indispensable. *Harvard Business Review* 89(10), 84–90, 92,153. PMID: 22111433.

Anchor 2 – Purpose

Arruda, W., Dib, D. & Bolles, R. (2013). *Ditch, Dare, Do: 3D Personal Branding for Executives (*1st ed). Trades Mark Press.

Alimujiang, A., MPH; Wiensch, A., MPH, Boss, J., MS et al, (2019) Association Between Life Purpose and Mortality Among US Adults Older Than 50 Years. *JAMA Network Open. (*2019) 2(5): e194270. doi:10.1001/jamanetworkopen.2019.4270.

Bombeck, E. (2003) *Eat less cottage cheese and more ice cream : thoughts on life from Erma Bombeck*; [illustrations by Lynn Chang]. Kansas City, Mo. : Andrews McMeel Pub. "The text of this book originally appeared in a newspaper column, 'If I had my life to live over, ' on December 2, 1979"–T.p. verso.

Covey, S. R. (2004). *The 7 habits of highly effective people: Restoring the character ethic* (Rev. ed). Free Press.

Frankl, V. E. (Viktor Emil, 1905–1997). (1962) *Man's Search for Meaning; an Introduction to Logotherapy.* Boston: Beacon Press.

Kashdan, T.B., & McKnight, P.E. (2009). Origins of Purpose in Life: Refining our Understanding of a Life Well Lived. *Psychological Topics*, (18), 303–313.

Nick, C. & Snook, S. (2014) From Purpose to Impact: Figure Out Your Passion and Put It to Work. *Harvard Business Review* 92 (5) 105–111; https://hbr.org/2014/05/from-purpose-to-impact.

O'Brien, D., Main, A., Kounkel, S & Stephan, A.R. (2019). Purpose is everything. How brands that authentically lead with purpose are changing the nature of business today. Deloitte Insights, 15 Oct. https://www2.deloitte.com/us/en/insights/topics/marketing-and-sales-operations/global-marketing-trends/2020/purpose-driven-companies.html.

Strecher, V. J. (2016). *Life on purpose: How living for what matters most changes everything.* Harper One, New York, NY.

Anchor 3 – Relationships

Clance, P.R., & Imes, S.A. (1978). The imposter phenomenon in high achieving women: Dynamics and therapeutic intervention. *Psychotherapy: Theory, Research & Practice, 15*(3), 241–247. doi.org/10.1037/h0086006.

Granovetter, M.S. (1973). The Strength of Weak Ties. *American Journal of Sociology, 78*(6), 1360–1380.

Huppert, M. (2017). Employees Share What Gives Them a Sense of Belonging at Work. https://www.linkedin.com/business/talent/blog/talent-engagement/employees-share-what-gives-them-sense-of-belonging-at-work.

Maister, D. H., Galford, R., & Green, C. (2001). *The trusted advisor*. Simon & Schuster.

Maslow, A. H. (1943). A theory of human motivation. *Psychological Review, 50*(4), 370–96.

Peterson, Jordan B., Doidge, Norman and Sciver E. Van. (2018). *12 Rules for Life: An Antidote to Chaos*. Toronto: Random House.

Sakulku, J. (2011). The Impostor Phenomenon. *The Journal of Behavioral Science, 6*(1), 75–97. doi.org/10.14456/ijbs.2011.6.

Wall, C. L. (2004). *The courage to trust: A guide to building deep and lasting relationships*. Oakland, CA: New Harbinger Publications.

Zak, P.J. (2017). The Neuroscience of Trust: Management Behaviours that Foster Employee Engagement, *Harvard Business Review*, Jan/Feb, 84–90.

Anchor 4 – Gratitude

Algoe, S. B. (2012), Find, Remind, and Bind: The Functions of Gratitude in Everyday Relationships. *Social and Personality Psychology Compass, 6*(6), 455–469. doi.org/10.1111/j.1751-9004.2012.00439.x.

Algoe, S. B., & Way, B. M. (2014). Evidence for a role of the oxytocin system, indexed by genetic variation in CD38, in the social bonding effects of expressed gratitude. *Social Cognitive and Affective Neuroscience, 9*(12), 1855–1861. doi.org/10.1093/scan/nst182.

Amin, A. (2014). The 31 benefits of gratitude you didn't know about: How gratitude can change your life. *Happier Human*. Retrieved from http://happierhuman.com/benefits-of-gratitude.

BIBLIOGRAPHY

Arnett, W. Will Arnett. Quotes from BrainyQuote.com. Retrieved September 14, 2023 from https://www.brainyquote.com/quotes/will_arnett_801179.

Bonnie, K. E., & de Waal, F. B. M. (2004). Primate Social Reciprocity and the Origin of Gratitude. In *The Psychology of Gratitude, Emmons, R. A. and McCullough, M. E. (Eds.)*, 213–229. Oxford University Press. doi.org/10.1093/acprof:oso/9780195150100.003.0011.

Brown. K. W., & Ryan, R. M. (2003). The Benefits of Being Present: Mindfulness and Its Role in Psychological Well-Being. *Journal of Personality and Social Psychology*, 84, 822-848.

Cheng, S., Tsui, P. K., & Lam, J. M. (2015). Improving mental health in health care practitioners: Randomized controlled trial of a gratitude intervention. *Journal of Consulting and Clinical Psychology*, 83, 177–186.

Chowdhury, M.R. (2021). The Neuroscience of Gratitude and How It Affects Anxiety & Grief, https://positivepsychology.com/neuroscience-of-gratitude/ 10/09/2021.

Conant, D. R., & Norgaard, M. (2011). *TouchPoints: Creating powerful leadership connections in the smallest of moments*. San Francisco, Calif: Jossey-Bass.

DeSteno, D., Li, Y., Dickens, L., & Lerner, J. S. (2014). Gratitude: A tool for reducing economic impatience. *Psychological Science*, 25(6), 1262–1267.

Dickens, L. R. (2017). Using gratitude to promote positive change: A series of meta-analyses investigating the effectiveness of gratitude interventions. *Basic and Applied Social Psychology*, 39(4), 193–208.

Dik, B. J., Duffy, R. D., Allan, B. A., O'Donnell, M. B., Shim, Y., & Steger, M. F. (2015). Purpose and meaning in career development applications. *The Counseling Psychologist*, 43(4), 558–585.

Disabato, D. J., Kashdan, T. B., Short, J. L., & Jarden, A. (2017). What Predicts Positive Life Events that Influence the Course of Depression? A Longitudinal Examination of Gratitude and Meaning in Life. *Cognitive Therapy and Research, 41(3),* 444–458. https://link.springer.com/article/10.1007/s10608-016-9785-xdoi.

Emmons, R. A., & Crumpler, C. A. (2000). Gratitude as a human strength: Appraising the evidence. *Journal of Social and Clinical Psychology*, 19(1), 56–69.

BIBLIOGRAPHY

Emmons, R. A., & McCullough, M. E. (2003). Counting blessings versus burdens: An experimental investigation of gratitude and subjective well-being in daily life. *Journal of Personality and Social Psychology, 84(2)*, 377–389. doi.org/10.1037/0022-3514.84.2.377.

Emmons, R.A. (2013). *Gratitude Works! A twenty-one-day Program for Creating Emotional Prosperity*. John Wiley & Sons.

Froh, J. J., Emmons, R. A., Card, N. A., Bono, G., & Wilson, J. A. (2011). Gratitude and the Reduced Costs of Materialism in Adolescents. *Journal of Happiness Studies*, 12(2), 289–302. doi.org/10.1007/s10902-010-9195-9.

Gleason, J. B., & Weintraub, S. (1976). The acquisition of routines in child language. *Language in Society*, 5(2), 129–136. doi.org/10.1017/S0047404500006977.

Jackowska, M., Brown, J., Ronaldson, A., & Steptoe, A. (2016). The impact of a brief gratitude intervention on subjective well-being, biology and sleep. *Journal of Health Psychology*, 21(10), 2207-2217.

Jans-Beken, L., Jacobs, N., Janssens, M., Peeters, S., Reijnders, J., Lechner, L., & Lataster, J (2020) Gratitude and health: An updated review, *The Journal of Positive Psychology*, 15:6, 743–782.

Kashdan, T. B., Mishra, A., Breen, W. E., & Froh, J. J. (2009). Gender differences in gratitude: Examining appraisals, narratives, the willingness to express emotions, and changes in psychological needs. *Journal of Personality*, 77(3), 691–730. doi.org/10.1111/j.1467-6494.2009.00562.x.

Knabb, J. J., Vazquez, V.E., Wang, K.T., & Pate, R.A. (2021). The Christian Gratitude Scale: An emic approach to measuring thankfulness in every season of life. *Spirituality in Clinical Practice*. Advance online publication. doi.org/10.1037/scp0000278.

Krause, N., & Hayward, R. D. (2014). Hostility, Religious Involvement, Gratitude, and Self-Rated Health in Late Life. *Research on Aging, 36(6)*, 731–752. doi.org/10.1177/0164027513519113doi.

Korb, A. (2015). *The upward spiral: Using neuroscience to reverse the course of depression, one small change at a time*. New Harbinger.

Layous, K., Nelson, S. K., Kurtz, J. L., & Lyubomirsky, S. (2017). What triggers prosocial effort? A positive feedback loop between positive activities, kindness, and well-being. *The Journal of Positive Psychology, 12*(4), 385–398. https:// doi.org/10.1080/17439760.2016.1198924.

Layous, K., Sweeny, K., Armenta, C., Na, S., Choi, I., & Lyubomirsky, S. (2017). The proximal experience of gratitude. *PLoS one, 12*(7), 1–26. doi.org/10.1371/ journal.pone.0179123.

Lin, C.-C. (2017). The Effect of Higher-Order Gratitude on Mental Well-Being: Beyond Personality and Unifactoral Gratitude. *Current Psychology, 36(1)*, 127–135. 10.1007/s12144-015-9392-0.

Liu, J., Gong, P., Gao, X., & Zhou, X. (2017). The association between well-being and the COMT gene: Dispositional gratitude and forgiveness as mediators. *Journal of affective disorders, 214*, 115–121. doi.org/10.1016/j. jad.2017.03.005.

Lyubomirsky, S., Dickerhoof, R., Boehm, J. K., & Sheldon, K. M. (2011). Becoming happier takes both a will and a proper way: An experimental longitudinal intervention to boost well-being. *Emotion, 11*(2), 391–402. doi.org/10.1037/a0022575.

McCullough, M. E., Emmons, R. A., & Tsang, J.-A. (2002). The grateful disposition: A conceptual and empirical topography. *Journal of Personality and Social Psychology, 82*(1), 112–127. doi.org/10.1037//0022-3514.82.1.112.

Ng, T. W. (2016). Embedding employees early on: The importance of workplace respect. *Personnel Psychology, 69*(3) 599-633.

Petrocchi, N., & Couyoumdjian, A. (2016). The impact of gratitude on depression and anxiety: the mediating role of criticizing, attacking, and reassuring the self. *Self and Identity, 15*(2), 191–205. doi.org/10.1080/1529886 8.2015.1095794.

Reckart, H., Huebner, E. S., Hills, K. J., & Valois, R. F. (2017). A preliminary study of the origins of early adolescents' gratitude differences. *Personality and Individual Differences, 116*, 44–50. doi.org/10.1016/j.paid.2017.04.020.

Seligman M.E. (2011) *Flourish: A Visionary New Understanding of Happiness and Well-Being*. New York, NY Free Press.

Seligman, M.E.P., Steen, T.A., Park, N., & Peterson, C. (2005). Positive psychology progress: Empirical validation of interventions. *Tidsskrift for Norsk Psykologforening, 42*, 874-884.

Stone, D. I., & Stone, E. F. (1983). The effects of feedback favorability and feedback consistency. *Academy of Management Proceedings* (00650668), 178–182.

Suchak, M., Eppley, T.M., Campbell, M.W., & de Waal, F.B.M. (2014). Ape duos and trios: spontaneous cooperation with free partner choice in chimpanzees. *PeerJ, 2*, e417. doi.org/10.7717/peerj.417.

Trivers, R. L. (1971). The Evolution of Reciprocal Altruism. *The Quarterly Review of Biology, 46*(1), 35–57. doi. org/10.1086/406755.

Tsang, J.-A., Carpenter, T. P., Roberts, J. A., Frisch, M. B., & Carlisle, R. D. (2014). Why are materialists less happy? The role of gratitude and need satisfaction in the relationship between materialism and life satisfaction. *Personality and Individual Differences, 64*(April), 62–66. doi. org/10.1016/j.paid.2014.02.009.

Tudge, J. R. H., Freitas, L. B. L., & O'Brien, L. T. (2016). The Virtue of Gratitude: A Developmental and Cultural Approach. *Human Development, 58*(4–5), 281–300. doi.org/10.1159/000444308.

Walker, J., Kumar, A., & Gilovich, T. (2016). Cultivating gratitude and giving through experiential consumption. *Emotion, 16*(8), 1126–1136.doi. org/10.1037/emo0000242.

Zahn, R., Garrido, G., Moll, J., & Grafman, J. (2014). Individual differences in posterior cortical volume correlate with proneness to pride and gratitude. *Social Cognitive and Affective Neuroscience, 9(11),* 1676–1683.

Anchor 5 – Health

Alda, M., Puebla-Guedea, M., Rodero, B. et al. (2016). Zen meditation, Length of Telomeres, and the Role of Experiential Avoidance and Compassion. *Mindfulness 7,* 651–659. doi.org/10.1007/s12671-016-0500-5.

Baek S. S. (2016). Role of exercise on the brain. *Journal of exercise rehabilitation, 12*(5), 380–385. doi.org/10.12965/jer.1632808.404.

Broderick, P.C. (2005). Mindfulness and Coping with Dysphoric Mood: Contrasts with Rumination and Distraction. *Cognitive Therapy and Research, 29*(5), 501–510. doi.org/10.1007/s10608-005-3888-0.

Brown, S. (2009). Discovering the Importance of Play through Personal Histories and Brain Images: An Interview with Stuart L. Brown. *American Journal of Play 1*(4), 399–412.

BIBLIOGRAPHY

Brown, S. (2009). *Play: How it Shapes the Brain, Opens the Imagination, and Invigorates the Soul*. (1st Ed) Avery.

Bryson, B. (2019). *The body: a guide for occupants*. (1st US ed.) New York: Doubleday.

Cafasso, J. (2017). *Why Do We Need Endorphins?* Healthline, 11 July. https://www.healthline.com/health/endorphins.

Creswell J. D., Myers H. F., Cole S. W., Irwin M. R. (2009). Mindfulness meditation training effects on CD4+ T lymphocytes in HIV-1 infected adults: a small randomized controlled trial. *Brain, Behavior and Immunity, 23*(2),184–188. doi: 10.1016/j.bbi.2008.07.004. PMID: 18678242; PMCID: PMC2725018.

Csikszentmihalyi, M. (1990). *Flow: The Psychology of Optimal Experience*. New York: Harper & Row.

Fluegge-Woolf, R.E. (2014). Play hard, work hard: Fun at work and job performance, Management Research Review, *(37)* 8, 682–705. doi.org/10.1108/MRR-11-2012-0252.

Geschwind, N., Peeters, F., Drukker, M., van Os, J., Wichers, M. (2011). Mindfulness training increases momentary positive emotions and reward experience in adults vulnerable to depression: a randomized controlled trial. *Journal of Consulting and Clinical Psychology. 79*(5), 618–628. doi: 10.1037/a0024595. PMID: 21767001.

Gordon, B. R., McDowell C. P., Hallgren, M., Meyer J. D., Lyons, M., Herring, M. P. (2018). Association of Efficacy of Resistance Exercise Training With Depressive Symptoms: Meta-analysis and Meta-regression Analysis of Randomized Clinical Trials. *JAMA Psychiatry, 75*(6), 566–576. doi:10.1001/jamapsychiatry.2018.0572.

Gray, P. (2015) .*Free to Learn: Why Unleashing the Instinct to Play Will Make Our Children Happier, More Self-Reliant, and Better Students for Life*. (1st Ed) Little Brown.

Guitard, P., Ferland, F., & Dutil, É. (2005). Toward a Better Understanding of Playfulness in Adults. *OTJR: Occupation, Participation and Health, 25*(1), 9–22. doi.org/10.1177/153944920502500103.

BIBLIOGRAPHY

Harris, R. (2019). *ACT made simple: an easy-to-read primer on acceptance and commitment therapy* (2nd ed.). New Harbinger Publications.

Hofmann, S. G., Sawyer, A.T., Witt, A. A., & Oh, D. (2010). The effect of mindfulness-based therapy on anxiety and depression: A meta-analytic review. *Journal of consulting and clinical psychology, 78*(2), 169–183. doi: 10.1037/a0018555. PMID: 20350028; PMCID: PMC2848393.

Hower, I. M., Harper, S. A., Buford, T. W. (2018). Circadian Rhythms, Exercise, and Cardiovascular Health. *Journal of circadian rhythms, 16*, 7. doi:10.5334/jcr.164.

Hülsheger, U. R., Alberts, H. J., Feinholdt, A., & Lang, J. W. (2013). Benefits of mindfulness at work: The role of mindfulness in emotion regulation, emotional exhaustion, and job satisfaction. *Journal of Applied Psychology, 98*(2), 310-325. doi:10.1037/a0031313.

Immordino-Yang, M. H., Christodoulou, J. A., & Singh, V. (2012). Rest Is Not Idleness: Implications of the Brain's Default Mode for Human Development and Education. *Perspectives on psychological science: a journal of the Association for Psychological Science, 7*(4), 352–364. doi: 10.1177/1745691612447308. PMID: 26168472.

Jabr, F. (2013). Why Your Brain Needs More Downtime. *Scientific American,* Oct. https://www.scientificamerican.com/article/mental-downtime.

Kaimal, G., Ray, K., & Muniz, J. (2016). Reduction of Cortisol Levels and Participants' Responses Following Art Making. *Art therapy: journal of the American Art Therapy Association, 33*(2), 74–80. doi.org/10.1080/07421656.2016.1166832.).

Kim, W. J, & Hur, M. H. (2016). Inhalation effects of aroma essential oil on quality of sleep for shift nurses after night work. *Journal of Korean Academy of Nursing, 46*(6), 769–779. doi.org/10.4040/jkan.2016.46.6.769.

Kotler, S. (2014). *The Rise of Superman: Decoding the Science of Ultimate Human Performance.* London, UK: Quercus Publishing.

Kotler, S. (2014). The Science of Peak Human Performance. *Time Magazine,* April 30.

Kotler, S. (2021). *The Art of Impossible: A Peak Performance Primer.* Harper Wave.

Kraemer, W.J., Ratamess, N. A., Hymer, W.C., Nindl, B. C., & Fragala, M. S. (2020). Growth Hormone(s), Testosterone, Insulin-Like Growth Factors, and Cortisol: Roles and Integration for Cellular Development and Growth With Exercise. *Frontiers in Endocrinology*, 11, 33. https://www.frontiersin.org/article/10.3389/fendo.2020.00033.

Kreider, T. (2012, June 30) The 'Busy' Trap, *New York Times*. https://opinionator.blogs.nytimes.com/2012/06/30/the-busy-trap/.

Lane , R.E. (2001). *The Loss of Happiness in Market Democracies.* New Haven: Yale University Press.

Levine, G.N., Lange, R.A., Bairey-Merz, C.N., Davidson, R.J., Jamerson, K., Mehta, P. K., ... & American Heart Association Council on Clinical Cardiology; Council on Cardiovascular and Stroke Nursing; and Council on Hypertension. (2017). Meditation and cardiovascular risk reduction: a scientific statement from the American Heart Association. *Journal of the American Heart Association,* 6(10), e002218.

Malinowski, P., Moore, A.W., Mead, B.R, & Gruber, T. (2017). Mindful Aging: The Effects of Regular Brief Mindfulness Practice on Electrophysiological Markers of Cognitive and Affective Processing in Older Adults. *Mindfulness, 8*(1), 78–94.
doi.org/10.1007/s12671-015-0482-8.

Okamoto-Mizuno, K., Mizuno, K. (2012). Effects of thermal environment on sleep and circadian rhythm. *Journal of Physiological Anthropology 31*, 14. doi.org/10.1186/1880-6805-31-14.

Pang, A.S-K. (2018). *Rest: Why You Get More Done When You Work Less.* Penguin UK.

Proyer, R. T., Tandler, N., & Brauer, K. (2019). Playfulness and Creativity: A Selective Review. In S. R. Luria, J. Baer, & J. C. Kaufman (Eds.), *Creativity and Humor* (pp. 43–60). Academic Press. doi.org/10.1016/B978-0-12-813802-1.00002-8.

Proyer, R. T. (2012). Examining playfulness in adults: Testing its correlates with personality, positive psychological functioning, goal aspirations, and multi-methodically assessed ingenuity. *Psychological Test and Assessment Modeling, 54*(2), 103–127. doi.org/10.5167/uzh-63532.

Proyer, R. T. (2013). The well-being of playful adults: Adult playfulness, subjective well-being, physical well-being, and the pursuit of enjoyable activities. *The European Journal of Humour Research*, *1*(1), 84–98. doi. org/10.7592/EJHR2013.1.1.proyer.

Quintana-Hernández, D.J., Miró-Barrachina, M. T., Ibáñez-Fernández, I. J., Pino, A. S., Quintana-Montesdeoca, M. P., Rodríguez-de Vera, B., Morales-Casanova, D., Pérez-Vieitez, M.delC., Rodríguez-García, J., & Bravo-Caraduje, N. (2016). Mindfulness in the Maintenance of Cognitive Capacities in Alzheimer's Disease: A Randomized Clinical Trial. *Journal of Alzheimer's disease: JAD*, *50*(1), 217-232. doi: 10.3233/JAD-143009. PMID: 26639952.

Robinson, L., Smith, M., Segal, J., and Shubin, J. (2021). The Benefits of Play for Adults. July www.helpguide.org/articles/mental-health/benefits-of-play-for-adults.htm.

Ströhle A. (2009). Physical activity, exercise, depression and anxiety disorders. *Journal of Neural Transmission* (Vienna, Austria: 1996), *116(6)*, 777–784. doi: 10.1007/s00702-008-0092-x.

Snyder-Mackler, N., Burger, J. R., Gaydosh, L., Belsky, D.W., Noppert, G.A., Campos, F.A., Bartolomucci, A., Yang, Y.C., Aiello, A.E., O'Rand, A., Harris, K.M., Shively, C.A., Alberts, S.C., Tung, J. (2020). Social determinants of health and survival in humans and other animals. *Science* (New York, N.Y.), *368*(6493). 10.1126/science.aax9553. Retrieved from https://hdl.handle.net/10161/21143.

University of Georgia. (2006, Nov. 8). Regular Exercise Plays A Consistent And Significant Role In Reducing Fatigue. *ScienceDaily*. Retrieved October 9, 2021 from www.sciencedaily.com/releases/2006/11/061101151005.htm.

Anchor 6 – Routines

Clear, J. (2018). *Atomic habits: tiny changes, remarkable results: an easy & proven way to build good habits & break bad ones.* New York: Avery, an imprint of Penguin Random House.

Currey, M. (2020). *Daily Rituals: How great minds make time, find inspiration, and get to work.* Picador.

Duhigg, C. (2014). *The Power of Habit: why we do what we do in life and business.* New York: Random House Trade Paperbacks.

BIBLIOGRAPHY

Dijksterhuis, A., Bos, M.W., Nordgren, L.F., & van Baaren, R.B. (2006). On making the right choice: The deliberation-without-attention effect. *Science* (New York, N.Y.), *311(5763)*, 1005–1007.

Mark, G., Gudith, D., Klocke, U. (2008). The cost of interrupted work: more speed and stress. CHI '08: Proceedings of the SIGCHI Conference on Human Factors in Computing Systems 6 April pp.107–110. https://www.ics.uci.edu/~gmark/chi08-mark.pdf.

Metin, U.B., Peeters, M.C.W., & Taris, T.W. (2018). Correlates of procrastination and performance at work: The role of having "good fit". *Journal of prevention & intervention in the community, 46*(3), 228–244. doi.org/10.1080/10852352.2018.1470187.

Murdock, M. Mike Murdoch Quotes from BrainyQuote.com. Retrieved September 14, 2023 from https://www.brainyquote.com/quotes/mike_murdock_185322.

Newport, C. (2016). *Deep work: rules for focused success in a distracted world.* New York: Grand Central Publishing.

Ofcom Communications Market Report. (2018). https://www.ofcom.org.uk/__data/assets/pdf_file/0022/117256/CMR-2018-narrative-report.pdf.

Sirois, F. M. (2015). Is procrastination a vulnerability factor for hypertension and cardiovascular disease? Testing an extension of the procrastination–health model. *Journal of behavioral medicine, 38*(3), 578–589.1-12. doi: 10.1007/s10865-015-9629-2.

Strick, M., Dijksterhuis, A., van Baaren, R. B. (2010). Unconscious-Thought Effects Take Place Off-Line, Not On-Line. *Psychological Science, 21*(4),484–488. doi.org/10.1177/0956797610363555 The Prince's Trust Youth Index. (2012). https://www.princes-trust.org.uk/Document_Youth-Index-2012.pdf.

Tice, D. M., & Baumeister, R. F. (1997). Longitudinal Study of Procrastination, Performance, Stress, and Health: The Costs and Benefits of Dawdling. *Psychological Science, 8*(6),454–458. doi:10.1111/j.1467-9280.1997.tb00460.x.

Wilson, D., Schooler, J., (1991). Thinking Too Much: Introspection can reduce the quality of preferences and decisions. *Journal of Personality and Social Psychology, 60*(2), 181–192.

Zalani, R. (2021). Screen Time Statistics: Your Smartphone is Hurting You. https://elitecontentmarketer.com/screen-time-statistics.

Zeigarnik, B. (1938). On finished and unfinished tasks. In W. D. Ellis (Ed.), *A source book of Gestalt psychology* (pp. 300–314). Kegan Paul, Trench, Trubner & Company. doi.org/10.1037/11496-025.

Anchor 7 – Resilience

Bajaj, B., Gupta, R. & Sengupta, S. (2019). Emotional Stability and Self-Esteem as Mediators Between Mindfulness and Happiness. *Journal of Happiness Studies, 20*, 2211–2226.

Ben-Avi, N., Toker, S., & Heller, D. K. (2018). "If stress is good for me, it's probably good for you too": Stress mindset and judgment of others' strain. *Journal of Experimental Social Psychology, 7*, 98–110. 10.1016/j.jesp.2017.09.002.

Campos, D., Cebolla, A., Quero, S., Bretón-López, J., Botella, C., Soler, J., García-Campayo, J., Demarzo, M., María Baños, R. (2016). Meditation and happiness: Mindfulness and self-compassion may mediate the meditation-happiness relationship. *The Journal of Personality and Individual Differences, 93*, 80–85.

Coutu, D. L. (2002). How resilience works. *Harvard Business Review, 80*(5), 46-50, 52, 55, passim. PMID: 12024758.

Dweck, C. S. (2006). *Mindset: The new psychology of success*. New York: Random House.

Johnson, S. (1998). *Who Moved My Cheese?: An Amazing Way to Deal with Change in Your Work and in Your Life*. New York: Putnam.

Milne, A. A., & Shepard, E. H. (1979). *Winnie-the-Pooh*. New York: Dell.

Sheldon, K. M., & Lyubomirsky, S. (2006). How to increase and sustain positive emotion: The effects of expressing gratitude and visualizing best possible selves. *The Journal of Positive Psychology, 1*(2), 73–82.

Shatte, A., Reivich, K. (2003) *The Resilience Factor: 7 Keys to Finding Your Inner Strength and Overcoming Life's Hurdles*. Harmony/Rodale.

Song, C., Ikei, H., Park B. J., Lee, J., Kagawa, T., & Miyazaki, Y. (2018). Psychological Benefits of Walking through Forest Areas. *International journal of environmental research and public health. 15*(12), 2804. doi.org/10.3390/ijerph15122804.

Vanderpol, M. (2002) Resilience: a missing link in our understanding of survival. *Harvard review of psychiatry, 10*(5), 302–306.

Vaillant, G. E. (2002). *Aging well: surprising guideposts to a happier life from the Landmark Harvard Study of Adult Development*. Boston: Little, Brown.

Vahidi, P. (2021) How to Bend, But Not Break – 7 Traits of Resilient People, NAMI Frontline Wellness. https://www.nami.org/Blogs/NAMI-Frontline-Wellness/2021/How-to-Bend-But-Not-Break-%E2%80%93-7-Traits-of-Resilient-People.

Youssef, C. M., & Luthans, F. (2007). Positive organizational behavior in the workplace: The impact of hope, optimism, and resilience. *Journal of Management, 33*(5), 774–800.

Additional Resources

The Flourishing Executives website is your portal to the most up-to-date information and resources related to building you or your team's 7 Anchors. Designed to complement this book, it has content which will allow you to:

- Assess your 7 Anchors through the questionnaire.
- Understand your 7 Anchors through the resource hub, which is continuously updating to include informative articles, resources and printable handouts, which build upon the content of this book.
- Get in touch with Trina Pitcher
- Improve you or your team's 7 Anchors by booking Trina Pitcher to run a workshop or program. Trina is entertaining, engaging and informative. She can tailor her content to suit your exact requirements and it can be delivered face to face or online. The 7 Anchors content is available in a wide variety of formats, ranging from one-hour keynotes to offsite retreats. The activities are guaranteed to leave attendees better equipped to live and lead a great life.
- Improve your 7 Anchors by engaging Trina as your personal executive coach. Trina is a highly experienced executive coach who can help you live and lead a great life.

To find out more please be in touch.
Visit **www.flourishingexecutives.com.au**
or use this QR code:

www.ingramcontent.com/pod-product-compliance
Lightning Source LLC
Chambersburg PA
CBHW010243010526
44107CB00062B/2673